Advance Praise for

THE LAW FIRM LIFE CYCLE

As lawyers, most of us learned the law but not the business of running a law firm. *The Law Firm Life Cycle* helps fill that gap as it is a roadmap that every law firm owner and aspiring owner should study.

Jonathan has lived through the good, the bad, and the ugly of firm formations, partnerships, and breakups. He's writing from the trenches. He has personally represented firms (and their lawyers) at every stage of their existence, from the moment of their creation to the pain of their dissolution.

There are many lessons to be learned from Jonathan's work in this space. Landmines to be avoided and opportunities to be taken advantage of.

I've spent my career helping entrepreneurial lawyers design practices that support the lives they want to live. Jonathan's work is a perfect complement to that mission. He reminds us that vision, structure, and preparation are necessities for survival, growth and happiness in this profession.

If you are thinking about starting a firm, joining with a partner, or planning your exit, read this book before you take your next step. It will save you heartache, money, and years of frustration. Jonathan has given our profession a rare gift: a candid, comprehensive guide to building and protecting the law firm that you and your clients deserve.

—**BEN GLASS**, Founder, Great Legal Marketing

The Law Firm Life Cycle distills the lessons every firm owner needs. Jonathan Hawkins shines a light on the partnership pitfalls that derail so many lawyers and offers practical guidance to build smarter, stronger firms.

—**RYAN MCKEEN**, Co-Founder of Best Era

Jonathan has written the definitive guide to the business of practicing law. Few lawyers understand the unique challenges of owning, growing, and sustaining a law firm with the depth and clarity that Jonathan brings. His counsel has been invaluable to me personally, and now he has distilled that same insight into a resource that every lawyer and law firm owner can rely on regardless of the stage they are at in the process. *The Law Firm Life Cycle* is more than a book, it is the essential playbook for building a firm with confidence, clarity, and longevity.

—**THOMAS TONA**, Founder & CEO of Tona Law

Scaling a law firm is hard, and the potential pitfalls are innumerable. Fortunately, here's a book from someone I trust about dealing with the practical growth of the firm and the hidden pitfalls from the perspective of the lawyer for law firm owners. Jonathan is among the most valuable resources you can have if you own or want to own a firm. Get this book. Read it. Save yourself a ton of headaches (and money).

—**CHARLEY MANN**, Founder of Law Firm Alchemy and Co-Founder of Red Kraken Creative

Finally, someone wrote the law firm owner's manual that law school forgot to give us. Jonathan Hawkins delivers the hard-won wisdom every entrepreneurial lawyer needs—from avoiding the "die at your desk" succession plan to building something that doesn't collapse the moment you take a vacation. If you want to run a law firm instead of letting it run you, this book is your new best friend.

—**TIM SEMELROTH**, Partner, RSH Legal

Most law firm owners think they're running a business. They're not. They're self-employed with overhead. *The Law Firm Life Cycle* shows you how to actually build a valuable law firm, not just a job with a cooler title. Read this book if you want freedom. Skip it if you don't.

—**BRIAN GLASS**, BenGlassLaw & Great Legal Marketing

We often learn by doing. Jonathan Hawkins shares his wisdom whether you're starting, growing, or winding down a law practice. Written in a conversational style, this book is both educational and enjoyable to read. Mr. Hawkins shares practical insights that will benefit entrepreneurial lawyers at any stage of their careers.

—**CATHERINE SANDERS REACH**,
Director of the Center for Practice Management,
North Carolina Bar Association

Jonathan brings a wealth of knowledge to the conversation of what it takes to run a purposeful and profitable law firm. With extensive experience representing law firms, he knows the ins and outs and all that can go wrong (and right) when you are building a firm. This book provides a roadmap to building a modern practice with intention and strategic foresight. Whether you are just starting out or looking to refine your existing practice, *The Law Firm Life Cycle* will help you navigate the complexities of law firm ownership with confidence and clarity.

—**NKOYO-ENE EFFIONG**, Director Law Practice
Management Program, State Bar of Georgia

Plenty of books tell you how to start a law firm, but few guide you through the entire journey—from launch to resolution. *The Law Firm Life Cycle* does exactly that. Written by someone who built his own firm from the ground up while also advising dozens of others, Jonathan offers practical, hard-earned lessons that only come from years in the trenches. As a law-firm owner in the Operations phase, I know I'll turn to this book again and again.

—TOM SPIGGLE, Founder of The Spiggle Law Firm

This is a must-have resource for all law firm owners. I wish this book was available when I launched my firm in 2012 as a solo; I would have saved a lot of time, headaches, and missteps. Fortunately, I now have it, the resources within, and Jonathan's expert guidance, as we continue to grow our firm, currently fourteen lawyers. I truly think it is invaluable for all entrepreneurial lawyers, whether at launch, during growth, or upon wind-up of a firm.

—KELLAM T. PARKS, Parks Zeigler, PLLC and The MOTIVATEd Lawyer, LLC

I had the privilege of working with Jonathan for over three years, and during that time he proved to be an invaluable advisor and partner. When I made the difficult decision to leave my first partnership, Jonathan was instrumental in guiding me through that transition with clarity and confidence. His counsel provided the stability I needed during a very uncertain time.

Afterward, as I entered into my subsequent partnership, Jonathan's expertise continued to be a cornerstone of our success. He provided our law firm with thoughtful guidance on a wide range of issues, particularly around employee relations and managing employer/employee friction. His ability to anticipate challenges, craft practical solutions, and align legal considerations with business goals gave us both peace of mind and a strong foundation to grow.

Perhaps most impressively, with Jonathan's counsel, we were able to avoid costly mistakes and implement sound strategies that ultimately saved our firm millions of dollars over the course of five years. His combination of legal acumen, strategic thinking, and genuine dedication make him a rare and trusted resource.

I wholeheartedly recommend Jonathan to any professional or firm seeking not just legal support, but a true partner in navigating both challenges and opportunities. This book is not only written from his extensive knowledge as a law firm owner but also working with law firms and helping them navigate the difficulties in owning a business. I highly recommend it.

—**LUIS SCOTT**, Founder of 8 Figure Firm

Jonathan Hawkins' *The Law Firm Life Cycle* is a practical roadmap for every stage of owning a law firm. From drafting airtight partnership agreements to avoiding disasters during firm breakups, Jonathan shares the hard-earned lessons every lawyer needs to know. I wish I had this book years ago.

—**PATRICK SLAUGHTER**, Founder of
The Small Firm Revolution

THE
LAW FIRM
LIFE CYCLE

THE LAW FIRM LIFE CYCLE
Counsel for Every Stage of Your Law Firm's Journey

ISBN: 978-1-964046-80-8

Expert
Press
www.ExpertPress.net

Editing by Elaina Robbins
Copyediting by Wendy Lukasiewicz
Proofreading by Heather Dubnick
Text design and composition by Emily Fritz
Cover design by Casey Fritz

THE
LAW FIRM
LIFE CYCLE

COUNSEL FOR EVERY STAGE
OF YOUR LAW FIRM'S JOURNEY

JONATHAN E. HAWKINS
THE LAW FIRM LAWYER™

To my family.
Thank you for being there with me every step of the way.

CONTENTS

INTRODUCTION

If you're reading this, we probably have some things in common.

Over the course of my career, I've clerked for a judge, been an associate in two law firms and a partner at two firms, and served as general counsel at both a law firm and in-house at a non-law business. I even took a sabbatical from law practice to serve as counsel to the Judiciary Committee of the Georgia House of Representatives. After all that, I started my own firm from scratch. I've seen many lawyers and staff come and go over the years, and I've had to hire and (unfortunately) fire people. I've even experienced a law firm dissolution from the inside.

You've probably been in at least one of those positions—likely more than one. And if you have, this book is for you. It's for law firm founders and owners, both current and aspiring.

You may be in the early stages of planning or have already launched your firm. You might be years into running your practice. Regardless of where you are on the path, we all share a common role: We are the leaders, decision-makers, and vision-holders of our firms.

Here's where we probably start to differ. Since 2009, I've been representing a specific clientele: you. Lawyers and law firms. I've worked with firms of every shape and size, from solo attorneys to firms with over two hundred lawyers. Firms that are virtual and distributed, firms with one office, firms with multiple offices across multiple states—I've done it all.

My lawyer clients have come from virtually every practice area: immigration, criminal, personal injury, insurance, defense, business, family, estate planning, employment, and niche areas most people have never heard of. I've worked with firms that bill hourly, those that use contingency fees, and those that use alternative fee arrangements (like flat or subscription fees). I've made a lot of mistakes along the way, and I've helped many lawyers and law firms who have made mistakes to regain their footing.

Here's what I've discovered after all that: Law firms have a life cycle, and if you're aware of the stages of this life cycle and what frequently happens during each stage, you can save yourself a lot of trouble.

Not all law firms get through every stage, but there are defined stages that you'll likely experience if you're a law firm owner.

LIFE CYCLE OF A LAW FIRM

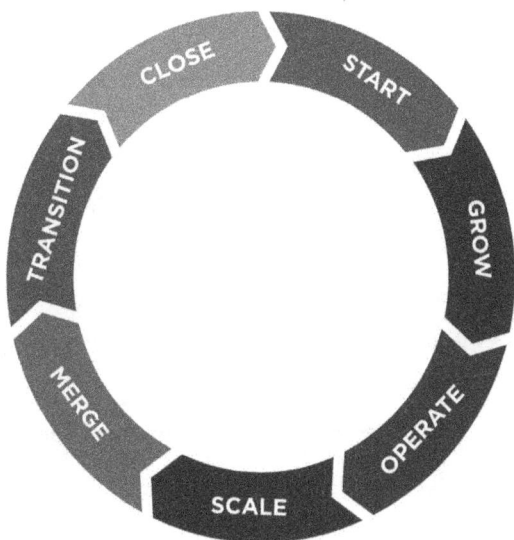

Start: Law firms are created in different ways and for different reasons—some contentious, some not. Whatever the case, there are initial steps you need to follow to set up your firm the right way, including choosing a business structure and creating a partnership agreement, if appropriate.

Grow: After a new firm is created, it hopefully gains traction. Work starts to roll in, and the founders get too busy to handle everything themselves. That means bringing in help and building support with attorneys, staff, and contractors. The complexity starts to build.

Operate: During this stage, firm owners really start to learn how to operate their business. They hone their processes, workflows, and other logistical elements so that the law firm catches its rhythm and begins to hum along. They may even begin to scale.

Merge: Law firm mergers happen for all sorts of reasons, from poor transition planning to strategic growth. Perhaps you are acquiring, or maybe you are being acquired. When you merge, you have a lot of complicated legwork ahead of you to minimize conflict and maximize efficiency and profits.

Transition: After operating for some time, law firm owners begin to think about transitioning—bringing in the next generation or two and setting the stage for exit.

Close: Whatever the reason, eventually most firms will end up closing. Shutting down a law firm isn't as simple as turning off the lights and locking the doors, especially for a firm that has been in existence a long time.

The only two stages that are inevitable are the starting and the closing. Some law firms start, never hit the growth stage, and end up closing. Others may grow and scale, then a breakup occurs and the firm closes, while the remnants go on to start new firms and the cycle begins again. But if things go according to plan, your law firm will progress through most of the stages in the life cycle of a law firm.

We learned a lot in law school, but we didn't learn about the business of law or how to run a law firm. And that is something I am genuinely passionate about. I love the *business* of law; it's a never-ending challenge and rarely boring. I also genuinely like my clients. I believe that lawyers, for the most part, are good people and great to work with. They are me, and I am them.

Representing lawyers and law firms—helping them protect and grow their practices in legal and ethical ways— is what I do. I get to meet other entrepreneurial lawyers and law firm leaders, compare stories, and learn from them. We get to grow together. My mission is to help law firm owners navigate this life cycle and thrive, whether they're just starting out or already in the thick of it.

I know all too well that owning and running a law firm can get lonely. While most law firm owners talk to and commiserate with other law firm owners, they often don't get the full picture. Some folks will share only the good, and many are reluctant to share the bad. Plus, even when other lawyers are willing to share their experiences, those experiences often won't apply to you. Every firm is different.

Many times, even if someone seems knowledgeable, you may not know the right questions to ask when it comes to running a law firm. To quote Donald Rumsfeld, there are "unknown unknowns."[1]

By virtue of my practice, I have seen a lot and bring that all to the table. I've worked with hundreds of lawyers and law firms. I have seen issues that arise, patterns that repeat, and challenges that blindside. I have worked with

---

1   Donald Rumsfeld, Interview by Deputy Inspector General for Investigations, Department of Defense, Office of Inspector General, U.S. Department of Defense, April 1, 2005, https://media.defense.gov/2006/Jun/30/2001774458/-1/-1/1/r_FOIA-Release-Rumsfeld-Transcript.pdf.

and understand firms that have been in every stage of the law firm life cycle.

In this book, you'll find practical advice, tools, and tips to reduce risk and build a foundation for long-term success in each stage of your firm's life cycle. I will also share knowledge and wisdom from law firm founders from all stages of the law firm life cycle who have been guests on my podcast, *Founding Partner Podcast*. By the time you reach the conclusion, I hope you feel empowered to anticipate obstacles and manage them with confidence.

When we ended our call, I started researching. Sure enough, there were a whole slew of law firm formations, changes, and breakups happening. Even more interestingly, I couldn't find any firms in Atlanta that specialized in this area. That was the seed, the genesis of the practice I have today.

Maybe your moment of inspiration came from a hole in the market, like the one my father pointed out to me. Maybe someone you know asked you to form a new partnership. Or maybe you didn't have much say in the matter at all—you were asked to leave without warning, or your firm blew up through no fault of yours.

Some start their firms straight out of law school. Others may leave a government position or a non-law business. But for most, immediately before starting their own firm, they are practicing law at an existing law firm. Hopefully, you've got time to prepare, but I've represented many who did not.

If it isn't forced upon you, this first step of the law cycle—the step where you're preparing to leave—can be both nerve-wracking and exciting. Owning and operating a firm may seem like the logical next step in a successful legal career. But the reality is far more nuanced.

Before you leave, you should weigh all the factors and make a calculated decision whether this is right for you. Once you've made the decision, you need to plan ahead and ensure you don't step on any land mines during your transition. From diligently adhering to the duties to your existing firm and clients, giving notice the right way, and

1. PRE-STEP—LEAVE

After becoming a lawyer, I always knew I would start own firm. I didn't know when, but I always knew. Some you may be the same, while some of you may have had intention of striking out on your own. Either way, you w somewhere before you started your firm.

I'm a second-generation attorney. Back in 2010, dad and I were both practicing; he was in Mobile, Alaba and I was in Atlanta, Georgia. I was a senior associate law firm at the time, primarily litigating business divo involving closely held non-law-firm businesses.

One night after work, I was chatting with my da the phone, and he mentioned he had finished handlin; fifth law firm breakup within the span of three years.

"There's a lot of these law firm breakups in Mol he said. "And Atlanta's ten times bigger. There's gotta bunch of these. You should look at it."

avoiding common pitfalls, there's a lot you can do to bring your new law firm into the world without a hitch.

Is Firm Ownership Right for You? The Entrepreneurial Factor

I've always had an enterprising spirit. Mine is a common story among entrepreneurs. As a kid, I sold baseball cards and candy at school. For undergrad, I went to Georgia Tech and got an industrial engineering degree, which has elements of a business degree. Originally, I thought I would go into finance or commercial real estate. Business has always been fun for me, so once I changed course, starting a law firm was probably inevitable.

This is not the case for everyone.

Business ownership can be rewarding, but it's not easy. Starting a firm means you're an entrepreneur and business owner instead of simply a lawyer. If you're business-minded like me, starting your own firm is great. But if your passion lies solely in being a high-level legal practitioner, launching a firm might not be the right path (unless you're forced into it).

Assuming you're not forced into the position of suddenly starting your firm, it is essential to pause and ask yourself: Do you really want to do this? Here are some factors to keep in mind.

Time Investment

Business owner and author Lori Greiner wrote, "Entrepreneurs are willing to work eighty hours a week to avoid working forty hours a week."[2] I couldn't agree more with that sentiment, especially in the legal world. For us, it's often more like leaving a sixty-hour job to work ninety hours. So if you're going to pursue this path, you need to know what you're getting yourself into and decide if it's what you want.

Don't jump in on a whim. For some, the solution isn't starting a firm at all; it might be joining another firm or even leaving the practice of law altogether. This is a big decision that requires clarity and conviction.

You will be spending a lot of time on your area of expertise, so choose something that genuinely interests you. Believe in your vision. Invest in it consistently. And keep going—even when no one's watching. Because one day, people will notice. What looks like overnight success will really be the result of years of quiet, determined effort.

Education

When I decided to explore representing lawyers and law firms, I started by immersing myself in the subject. I read several major treatises and many shorter practice area books cover to cover. Then came the law review articles—hundreds of them. I followed that with case law from across the country, building a deep and nuanced understanding of the field.

As I studied, I created my own digest files—summaries, notes, and frameworks that helped me internalize the material. Those files became a foundational resource I still

---

2   Lori Greiner, *Invent It, Sell It, Bank It!: Make Your Million-Dollar Idea into a Reality* (New York: Ballantine Books, 2014), 258.

rely on today. Of course, that was before all the education needed to run a business.

You already went to law school, but if you're going into a new practice area, you will need to educate yourself fully on that area. Additionally, you will need to learn how to run a successful business. This can be fascinating, but it's also a huge investment of time. You can help yourself out by getting a head start while you're at your current job.

Diverse Responsibilities

Starting a firm means shifting a considerable portion of your time toward operational and administrative tasks. You will find yourself immersed in activities like recruiting, hiring, managing, training, setting up technology, opening bank accounts, and even ordering office supplies.

At an established firm, if you need a pen or pad, you walk down the hall and pick one up. Initially, when you launch your own firm, you're the one responsible for stocking the supply closet. These tasks are largely invisible when you're at an established firm, but when you're the only person working, everything changes. You have to be prepared for that.

Initial Capital

Without adequate savings or access to credit, the initial months can quickly become stressful. Do you have enough money socked away to float your business for the first few months or maybe longer? If not, do you have access to a business loan? Before you leave your current position, build your war chest or get that line of credit.

Client Acquisition Plan

Maybe you're fortunate enough to start your firm with a handful of clients (which is pretty common). But those matters will eventually wrap up, and when they do, you need a steady pipeline to sustain the business. That means you must have an explicit plan for how you'll bring in new clients.

Getting the ball rolling on client acquisition isn't easy. I began the process of building a strong marketing strategy for Law Firm GC years before I pulled the trigger. As I researched this area of practice, I began contacting other lawyers, sharing what I was learning, and listening to their insights. I wrote articles, launched a blog, and committed to publishing weekly content for three years straight. I built an email list and sent out regular updates—something I still do to this day. I also spoke at events, offered pro bono help to colleagues, and took on every opportunity to apply what I was learning.

All this happened outside of my billable hours. No one asked me to do it. No one tracked it. But I knew it mattered.

Eventually, the work paid off. My first client came through. Then another. And another. Over time, what started as a personal project became a thriving practice.

You have to be prepared to do this legwork early on. If you're not confident in your ability to find clients, you will need to learn how. Because without clients, your firm won't survive.

Spouse/Family Buy-In

You need more than your own buy-in to start a firm; you need your family to prepare themselves as well. Launching a firm isn't a solo endeavor, and your support system must be aligned with the potential sacrifices ahead. If you're skipping paychecks or draining family finances to fund the new firm, your spouse or family has to be part of the decision to do so. If you're sacrificing evenings, weekends, and vacation time, it's better to get everyone on board beforehand. If you're stressed out later, these conversations will be insurmountably more difficult.

That last one can be a real hurdle. I remember convincing my wife to give me a shot when I decided to leave and start my own firm: "Trust me," I told her. "I'll do better than where I am now." I was confident. But because of the way law firm cash flow works—the billing cycle, payment delays—it took many months before I was back to my previous income. That's significant for anyone, but it's especially significant if you have two young kids and a spouse to support.

After three months, my wife asked me, "What are you doing? You said you would be doing better. What's going on here?" She was right. It wasn't going exactly like I had said it would. But I replied, "Hold on. Just hold on." Because I believed in it. I knew what was coming.

Sure enough, I eventually turned the corner, and the cash flow grew. That momentum continued. By late 2024, we had grown into a team of six attorneys and three staff members. We're still growing. But I wish I had done a better job beforehand explaining to my family about that potentially prolonged buffer period; it would have saved us both a lot of tossing and turning. That said, because I'm continuing to reinvest to grow, I still have moments stressing about cash flow.

By carefully weighing each of these points, you can make sure you're not making a mistake before you start investing money and time into your new firm.

What's Your Vision?

Once you've decided that law firm ownership is indeed right for you, it's time to think about your vision. What do you want your law practice to look like? There is no "right" answer—this is all about what is right for you.

What you want may be different from what someone else wants. There are many folks out there telling you what you should want, but you need to ignore them and decide for yourself.

We're all bombarded with messages about how to live our lives: We should be hustling more, we should be scaling our business, we should be taking cold plunges every morning. I'm all about exploring, but just because something may work for someone else doesn't mean it will work for you. A great resource to help you decide what you truly want is the book *Vivid Vision* by Cameron Herold.

Figure out what you want—what you really want—and what works for you. Then ignore the noise and build your vision, not someone else's.

Take me, for example. I have a clear vision: I want to build a national firm. I want to grow this niche practice to eventually operate in multiple states. This directly informs the decisions I make. It means that, at some point, I will open an office in another state. And then another. And to make that happen, I have to go meet people in these other states. It's going to be a long process to make that happen, but I know where I'm going, and I know what I need to do to get there.

What practice area will you handle? This is a substantial part of your vision for your firm. A lot of lawyers come to me when they're starting their own firms and say, "I don't know what I want to do. I might do a little bit of criminal, I'll do a little bit of family law, maybe I'll do some plaintiff contingency car wreck work." They take on whatever comes in the door, which is a good way to stress yourself out because you're constantly learning new practice areas. It's also a recipe for disaster—never attaining expertise in any one practice area means you may end up committing malpractice.

You would be much better off focusing on one or two practice areas. That way, you're not chasing shiny objects everywhere and running yourself ragged. It's also easier to get referrals this way. You can tell other lawyers, "I do divorce work. If you see anything, send it to me."

An unmistakable vision of where you want to go guides all your decisions. Without that vision, you can end up drifting in a direction you never intended to go. You can work hard, build something, and still wake up one day and realize you went wrong somewhere. That happens more often than people admit.

Podcast Feature: Ben Glass on Vision

My friend Ben Glass, founder of BenGlassLaw and Great Legal Marketing, has been a leader in the entrepreneurial law firm space for decades. He specializes in helping lawyers create a better life for themselves, fostering happiness for themselves and their family without increasing the chaos that oftentimes comes with growth. As such, he thinks a lot about vision, both for himself and for Great Legal Marketing members. His approach to designing a law practice is the philosophy I believe in, so I pulled some of his thoughts from our *Founding Partner Podcast* episode to share with you.

Design Your Life First, Then Your Firm

Ben's core philosophy is to build your firm around the life you want, not the other way around. "There's a path to happiness in the profession," he told me. "Your future is not in working in a big firm for somebody else. You have a right to live your life as you want it. You get to design a practice that you want and that's great for you."

Ben believes that although practicing law is stressful, you can design it to be an enjoyable part of your life, factoring in work-life balance. "There is another way. There's a whole bunch of us who are enjoying the practice," he tells me. "Making more money . . . that's important. But what does the money get you? The time freedom, the freedom to do things with your family that you wanna do."

Ben believes that every lawyer should define their personal vision of "perfect" and reverse engineer their firm to support it. For example, we talked about lawyers who love being in trial but detest doing all the busywork involved with it. "If that's their definition of perfect, then great," he said. "They need to surround themselves with people who can go get cases, bring in experts, handle the paperwork so they can focus on being in trial. We don't judge whether someone should be doing legal work or trying cases. That's not our call. What we do is help lawyers who've made that decision—who know where their time and energy are best spent—get there."

Growth Isn't One-Size-Fits-All

Growth is likely part of your vision, and just like vision, it differs from firm to firm. "For some people, growth means I wanna have multi-offices, multi-location offices," Ben explains. "You might say, 'I wanna have fifty or a hundred people under my roof working.' And of course, in America, there are firms with lots more people under their roofs."

He also brought up how crucial family buy-in is for vision, especially when it comes to growth. And when it comes to family, he is walking the walk: Ben has been married since 1982 and has nine children, one of whom now helps him run his business. "It's been important that our growth at BenGlassLaw and Great Legal Marketing is aligned with what we want to do as a family," he told me. "So what does perfect look like for you and your spouse and your family? Because if the lawyer is happy and wants multi-city location growth, but the spouse is like, 'No, this is driving me crazy.' . . . Let's make sure that you are aligned as a family first. That's a big thing."

Preparing to Leave

Once you're sure you want to start your own law firm, it's time to start planning. If you're at an existing law firm, there are important duties and restrictions that lawyers must be aware of before leaving. Part of this is knowing who to tell—and knowing who not to tell.

Keeping Quiet: The Pitfalls of Telling the Wrong (or Too Many) People

It can be difficult to keep your exciting news quiet, but in the early stages of telling others about your decision to leave, you have to be selective about who you tell and when you tell them. So many attorneys make the mistake of talking too openly about their plans before they officially leave. Many lawyers make avoidable missteps during this critical pre-departure phase that compromise their reputations, finances, or legal standing, and primary among those is premature disclosure.

There's an old saying worth remembering: Loose lips sink ships. This goes beyond duty to your firm or clients; you never know who might be listening, and an offhand remark can circulate and reach the wrong ears.

For instance, two attorneys I know had been planning to exit a firm and start their own partnership for several months. (All identifiers have been changed or omitted in the stories in this book.) They were preparing to launch in January and had already been in discussions with real estate brokers, insurance providers, and banks. It seemed like everything was going according to plan.

Weeks before the new partners were ready to inform their firm of their decision, the managing partner in their current firm summoned them into a meeting.

"We know you're planning to leave," the partner said. The meeting ended abruptly, and those two attorneys were out of the firm the same day. Their preparations—though strategic—hadn't remained confidential, and their timeline accelerated.

Many lawyers plan to depart their firms after receiving their year-end bonus. It routinely happens every January.

Leaving after getting paid a bonus that has been earned isn't typically the basis for a claim, but you should still be careful not to make misrepresentations.

In short, leave smart. Maintain confidentiality. Be respectful. Avoid cutting corners. And most of all, remember that you don't want to burn any bridges on your way out.

Who Do I Tell First: My Firm or My Clients?

Generally speaking, you should give notice to your firm that you're leaving before telling any clients. Always check your jurisdiction's rules, but most ethics rules and opinions agree on that. It's not a hard-and-fast rule; it exists on a spectrum, and it all depends on what kind of clients you cater to.

On one end of that spectrum are consumer-facing clients who are often individuals—think personal injury clients or family law clients. In those situations, it's pretty obvious that notice should go to the firm first before any contact is made with the client.

On the other end of the spectrum are what I would call highly sophisticated clients. Think of a Fortune 50 company where the client contact is the general counsel. In those cases, the general counsel will probably want to have input on where their legal work is going.

Let's put this in context. Imagine that you've accepted a job offer from another firm and notified your current firm that you're leaving. Then you inform the general counsel of the Fortune 50 client that you're moving to this new firm.

"We don't like that firm," they tell you. "We're not sending our work there." Now you're stuck.

In that scenario, it might make more sense to talk to the client first, as keeping that one important client may be worth staying put. That's a judgment call and fact-specific, but in cases like that, giving the client a heads-up first could be justified.

Whether you tell them before or after your firm, you must keep your clients reasonably informed about the status of their legal matters. When your departure from a law firm may affect a client's case or representation, the client needs to know. Both the departing attorney and the law firm must ensure that the facts surrounding the departure are accurately and honestly communicated to clients, as any misrepresentation regarding your departure would violate professional conduct standards.

Remember, cases don't belong to a law firm or lawyer. They belong to the clients. Clients get to choose who their lawyer is. If a client wants to leave, the lawyer has to let them go. That's why the client relationship matters. Always nurture the relationship. Make it so the client never wants to leave.

Duties to Firm and Duties to Clients

Whether you've started telling people or not, you have certain duties while you're still at your current firm. This includes duties to your current firm and to your clients. Sometimes those duties may conflict.

Duties to Firm

You likely already know that lawyers owe certain legal duties to their current law firms. These obligations arise from a combination of sources: fiduciary principles, common law, ethical rules, and, often, written agreements between the parties.

Duties of Non-Partners Versus Partners

Let's say you're an associate at your current firm. Your duty to your firm is grounded in principles of employment and agency law. You're expected to provide faithful service and prioritize the interests of the firm while you work there, even if you've decided to leave.

If you're a partner, these responsibilities are much greater. Partners are in a fiduciary relationship with one another and are expected to act with the utmost good faith and the highest standard of loyalty. Just like an associate or other employee attorney, you must continue to uphold the highest standards of work until your last day at your current firm. But unlike an employee attorney, if your firm asks you directly if you're leaving, you cannot misrepresent your intentions. In addition, if you know you will be leaving and the firm is making a significant financial decision, like signing on to a new long-term lease, under the impression you will be there, you have an affirmative obligation to let the firm know before it enters into that lease.

Acting in the Best Interests of Your Current Firm

Your duty to your current firm goes beyond telling your partner or partners that you are planning on leaving. Depending on the practice, certain behaviors are considered improper and could be breaches of duty. There are also important ethical considerations around notifying clients.

Let's say your current firm uses billable hours. Some lawyers might be tempted to delay invoicing or recording that work so they can claim it under the new firm instead. This is improper. The work was done at the original firm and was compensated there, so reassigning it to the new firm amounts to a breach of duty.

Here's another example that applies to both hourly and contingency firms. If a lawyer receives a new client referral shortly before leaving, they might be tempted not to inform the current firm about the client. It would be easy to tell the client that you're leaving and encourage them to wait to sign the case under the new firm. Holding the client this way and signing them up with the new firm before officially leaving the old firm is improper and constitutes a breach.

Unfortunately, this happens all the time. In one notorious case, a firm based in Boston had a Seattle office led by a managing partner. That managing partner—let's call her Mindy—was paid by the firm. She was actively doing work and receiving clients from the firm. Then, the firm—let's call it Firm A—found out that Mindy had set up a competing law firm. She was marketing that separate firm while still employed at Firm A, trying to generate cases for her competing firm during this time.

This was a huge problem and a clear breach of duty of loyalty. Interestingly, Mindy never successfully signed up any clients for the competing firm, so she didn't make any money from it.

Mindy's former firm sued her for damages. The trial court initially ruled that since no damages were proven, there was no claim. On appeal, however, the court overturned this decision and ruled that Mindy had to repay all the money she earned from the original firm during the time she breached her duty. Trying to compete was enough to hold her liable to pay back all compensation received while breaching her duty. That is not a situation you want to be in.

Duties to Clients

There are duties you owe to your current firm, and then there are duties owed to your clients. The key here is that both the departing lawyer and the firm owe a duty to the client. These departures can get heated, and when they do, it's easy for both sides to get so angry that the client's interests end up ignored. As difficult as it may be, the attorneys must ensure the client is protected.

You know well that attorneys are required to provide competent representation, which includes the legal knowledge, skill, thoroughness, and preparation reasonably necessary for the matter at hand. Additionally, the duty of confidentiality prohibits lawyers from disclosing any information gained in the course of the professional relationship unless the client has given informed consent. Even during all the tumult of transition, you have to keep these things in mind.

Generally speaking, the duty to the client should prevail over any duty to the firm. The client's representation should not be disrupted in such a way that the client is harmed. Say a hearing is coming up next week, and only the departing attorney is familiar with the file. If the firm locks that attorney out and denies access to the file, the client's case could suffer. If something goes wrong, both the firm and the attorney could be held liable by the client.

In cases like that, even if the relationship has gotten tense and the firm is tempted to block access, the client's well-being must be prioritized. That might mean the firm has to grant access to case files. It might also mean that you, as the departing attorney, choose not to disclose your intent to leave until after this client's case is concluded.

Another point worth emphasizing: The client gets to decide who represents them. If the client says, "I want to go with the departing attorney," the firm must respect that and release the file. A client's file can't be held hostage; this could harm the client and expose the firm to liability. On the flip side, if the client chooses to stay with the firm, you must respect that decision. Continuing to interfere at that point could cause serious problems.

No matter how complicated and delicate client transitions can be during a lawyer's departure from a firm, everyone involved must keep the client's best interests front and center.

Worst-Case Scenario: Facing a Lawsuit

Even when you do everything right when departing from a firm, hurt feelings and disputes may lead to a lawsuit. A departing attorney who takes clients may represent a significant financial loss, presenting an issue for the firm. The law firm may refuse to pay money owed, presenting a problem for the attorney. The resulting tension often translates into legal threats—and sometimes into actual litigation.

In my experience, most of these situations resolve themselves short of a lawsuit either through negotiation or a formal mediation. But sometimes, the stakes are too high, and the parties are too far apart to reach an agreement. Formal legal action is then inevitable.

As you know, litigation can be expensive, time-consuming, and emotionally draining for all involved. Litigation is different when you are a party than when you are the lawyer for a party; the stress and sleepless nights can be tough. After litigating these types of disputes for many months, I have had tough trial attorney clients tell me that they have a newfound appreciation for what their clients go through. If you find yourself in litigation over your departure, remember that this chapter of your career will eventually end. Before you know it, you will be able to move on and start anew.

Plan, Prepare, Prevail

I still remember that phone call with my dad—the one where he suggested I think about starting my own firm. That was a turning point for me, and it set me on a path that's been challenging and deeply rewarding.

Maybe you're standing at a similar crossroads right now. Maybe you've already made the decision to leave, or maybe you're still weighing your options. Or perhaps you have little say in the matter and have no choice but to start something on your own. For those with no time to prepare, I've put together an Emergency Law Firm Start-Up Checklist. You can access it in the resources section of *The Law Firm Life Cycle* landing page: https://www.lawfirmgc.com/life-cycle-resources/.

Whatever your situation, know this: The decision to step away from a firm, whether by choice or circumstance, isn't only a legal or logistical one; it's also personal. It involves not only you, but also your clients, your current firm, and even your family. It's the beginning of something entirely new.

The more intentional you are in this early stage, the better positioned you'll be to build something that reflects your values, your goals, and your vision for the future. By carefully considering your duties to your current firm and clients, towing the line when it comes to giving notice to the right people in the right order, and avoiding common pitfalls, you can set yourself up for the best transition possible to law firm ownership.

2. THE BIRTH OF A LAW FIRM—START

Every law firm has an origin story. Mine is a little different from most.

My entrepreneurial streak tempted me, a few times in my career, to stop practicing law. I feel like many lawyers go through that. Before I made partner at my first firm, I had a lot of friends doing business or other non-law ventures. This was before the Great Financial Crisis—before the real estate crash—and I was genuinely interested in what they were doing. I thought maybe I wanted to get into that world too.

Tim, a friend from college and also a longtime client, had always kicked around business ideas with me. We even tried some things on the side. He was in business with his dad and brother in real estate. Eventually, after their last project together, Tim's dad and brother bowed out. Tim called me and said, "I want to keep going. Do you have any interest in joining me? I don't know what your role will be, but I know it'll be great." I said, "Sure. That sounds fun."

Tim said he could pay me only a small salary to start. So we struck a deal: I would work part time with him, and I would keep a part-time law practice. I basically had two part-time jobs: one a non-law start-up and the other my small law firm.

When I left my firm as I transitioned to this new work arrangement, I cut a huge chunk of my practice and left it there. I kept the core piece—representing lawyers and law firms—but my new firm was very much a lifestyle practice, designed to make room for this new venture.

I learned a ton from Tim's new venture. I saw business up close. Real business. Tim was an experienced entrepreneur, and he was never afraid to take calculated risks. He hired early to build out infrastructure. He would borrow large sums of money to invest, with a strategy to recoup it on the back end.

That mindset stuck with me. Lawyers are often scared to hire people, scared to invest. They want to take all the money out of the firm at the end of the year instead of reinvesting for growth. But I got to watch someone do it differently—and successfully—in real time.

My original plan, when I joined that company, was to eventually shut down my law practice and go into business with Tim full time. That was the vision. But things changed. Our projects got bigger, timelines stretched longer, and then COVID-19 hit, which upended everything.

I loved being in business with Tim, but I had a serious problem. My destiny wasn't in my control when I worked for someone else. It wasn't even fully in Tim's hands—it was tied to the economy, interest rates, and other factors.

Meanwhile, something unexpected was happening. Work kept coming into my legal practice. The years I had spent building relationships, serving people well, and staying visible began paying off. Despite not marketing or advertising, I kept getting referrals, and the work kept showing up.

That's when I realized people needed what I had to offer. I started to get excited about the law business again. So Tim and I agreed that I needed to leave the business, we shook hands, and I dedicated myself to Law Firm GC.

Whether your road is more straightforward than mine or just as winding, starting a law firm comes with a lot of important decisions. The most important is deciding on a vision for your firm. Another critical one is whether you decide to go it alone or form a firm with one or more other lawyers. Each path offers its own advantages and challenges, and it's important to weigh these carefully at the outset. Your choice heavily affects the steps you will need to take to get your new firm set up.

In this chapter, we'll examine the pros and cons of partnership and solo firms so you can decide which is right for you. I'll also share some special considerations when choosing partners and creating partnership agreements. By setting everything up correctly, you can help your brand-new law firm hit the ground running.

Solo Versus Partnership: Which Is Right for You?

Why start your own solo practice versus joining forces with someone and starting a partnership? It depends a lot on you, how you work, and what you're looking for.

This is such a pivotal decision that it's worth comparing and contrasting solo and partnership structures. I've owned a solo firm and been in partnerships, and each comes with specific advantages and disadvantages. Before you decide whether to start out on your own or go in with a partner, read this section and think about what best suits your needs.

Solo Firms

First, I want to emphasize that I'm talking about true solo firms here. There's a difference between a true solo practice and a solely owned firm.

A true solo firm has one attorney doing everything. If you're getting started, that's probably what you can expect (at least for the first few months). A solely owned firm, on the other hand, is a firm with a single owner but a team of employees, often including attorneys.

As I write this today, I'm the sole owner of my firm. I also have a team of five other attorneys and several staff. So for now, my firm is a solely owned firm, but I still have plenty of help.

In this section, though, we will be considering the true start-up scenario: You out on your own without a team to support you. If you're starting a solo firm by yourself, these are the advantages and disadvantages you'll need to consider.

Advantages

Solo firms are, in many respects, less complicated than partnerships. From forming a legal entity to deciding where to operate, the logistics are straightforward compared to the intricate dynamics of a partnership.

If you own a solo firm, you get to make all the decisions. You don't have to ask permission or get buy-in from anybody. You decide the vision and direction of the firm and how much or how little you're going to work. There's a lot more flexibility, and there are fewer commitments. You can move fast.

And if you're doing well, you have no one to split profits with. I'm still the sole owner of my firm, but things are different now that I have a team working for me. When I was truly by myself, I didn't have to work as much to make a decent living. My profit margins were through the roof because of low overhead.

With a laptop, an internet connection, and a bar license, you can do your work wherever you are as a solo firm. It's not universal—you may have to go to court, for example—but you don't need a lot of paying clients to make a good living. Therefore, if you can figure it out, being solo is pretty nice.

Disadvantages

Being a solo law firm owner isn't all high profits and smooth sailing. There are challenges.

First, it can be difficult to get the business model right. Plenty of solo attorneys barely scrape by. That's often because they haven't figured out the basics: how to get clients, how to get clients to pay them, and/or how much to charge their clients.

Second, since you're the only one in the business, the business rests entirely on your shoulders. If you're not doing the work, no one will. If you've got too much work, you have to work your tail off—day, night, and weekends—because you have no help. That's the crux of the scalability problem with solo law firms. Until you start hiring, you can only handle as many cases as you personally can take on.

Keep in mind that these disadvantages apply to a true solo practice. As you grow, you can hire help and find a better balance. Ultimately, if you get through it all, a solely owned firm can be rewarding. But, at first, the stress levels are higher with a solo firm.

Partnerships

If doing everything yourself sounds more stressful than freeing, you may want to consider a partnership. Like solo firms, partnerships come with distinct advantages and disadvantages. You should weigh these carefully before you decide to go into business with someone else.

Advantages

In a partnership, you share risk. If one partner is doing well and the other isn't, it evens out over time. You share the workload, the burden of growing the firm, the overhead. This puts less pressure on you.

Also, since you have a partner, you don't have the onus to do everything yourself. If you get sick, you can take a day off and lean on your partner. If you're overwhelmed, you can ask for help in a way that a solo firm owner can't at first. It's easier to take a real vacation.

Finally, there's size and scale. Theoretically, the pie gets bigger, and everyone gets a piece. You might also diversify into different practice areas, which helps manage risk. This is why most of the largest, most profitable law firms are partnerships. There's only so much you can do on your own.

Disadvantages

There's a trade-off between speed, clarity, and decision-making when comparing a solely owned firm with a partnership. In a solo firm, you get to make all the decisions. In a partnership, you have to agree with your partner or partners, so it can be harder to make decisions. If you don't have a clear leader, you need to create committees and decision-making by consensus.

The barriers to decision-making can have a profound effect on a law firm. Big decisions may never get made or may take months or years. If you disagree on a decision, it might keep getting pushed off, or someone might eventually say, "I don't care; just choose." Therefore, if speed and the ability to make decisions are important to you, a solo firm may be a better fit.

Also, profit margins generally go down in a partnership. You're trading profit for scale. That's the reality in any business. When I was truly solo, I was working part time with 90 percent profit margins. If you have a partnership with a team, you have to think about payroll, distributing work, managing stress—all of it. You might make about the same as you would in a solo law firm, but with far more complexity and moving parts.

Naming Your Firm: Trade Name or Traditional Name?

For many years, most jurisdictions prohibited trade names for law firms. Those that did allow them required that a name of at least one equity owner be included. Years ago, in Georgia, my firm was called Law Firm GC (Hawkins), LLC. Catchy, right?

Thankfully, many states have rolled that back. Trade names and branding are now mostly allowed, although you should check your jurisdiction to be sure. If it is permissible in your area, the question is clear: Should you use a trade name or stick to the traditional route?

This question is somewhat controversial because lawyers can be a funny bunch. Some of us are traditionalists who want our names on the door. But not everyone feels that way. More and more firms are moving toward trade names instead of partner names. So if you're starting a new firm, you need to think about which route you want to take.

If you've been around for fifteen years with an established name and reputation, then suddenly changing your name could hurt your brand. But if you're starting from scratch, a trade name is a smart move. (That's why I have one.) We'll get into this further in chapter 6, but for now, here are three reasons why using a trade name makes sense:

1. You avoid the naming battle. I've seen this too many times. A new partner joins and wants their name on the door. Then the questions ensue: Whose name goes first? Why isn't my name there? Soon, you've got a fight over something that doesn't matter. You can avoid the drama entirely with a trade name.

2. You have fewer headaches when things change. Partners come and go. When someone's name is part of the brand, their departure means rebranding—new name, new URL, new signage, new everything. It's a giant pain, and a trade name means you'll never have to deal with that.

3. You get more value on exit. If the firm is named after you, it may make the difficult task of selling a law firm even harder. A trade name makes the business more transferable because ownership can change without needing to change the brand.

That's why, if you're starting out or still in the early stages of your firm, I strongly encourage you to consider a trade name. It might save you a lot of unnecessary conflict and hassle down the road. And if you develop a strong brand, you increase the value of your firm.

You've Got to Start Somewhere

I had a podcast guest on recently who told me they used folding card tables as desks when they were launching their firm. I thought that was such a quirky detail but also brilliant in its simplicity. And that guest isn't alone. When Jeff Bezos was first getting started, he wanted to save money on desks. So instead of buying standard office furniture, he went to Home Depot, bought some doors, and turned them into desks. That do-it-yourself mentality became a tradition at Amazon even after the company made it big.[3]

Maybe makeshift desks aren't what everyone envisions when they think of starting a business, but honestly, I think it's spot on. The truth is that you don't need a mahogany desk to get going. You just need to start. These days, you only need a computer, an internet connection, and a bar license, especially if you choose to start a solo practice.

That's literally how I started. I didn't have a logo, a website, or an office. I did have a laptop, Wi-Fi, and my

---

3   Neal Karlinsky and Jordan Stead, "How a Door Became a Desk, and a Symbol of Amazon," About Amazon, January 17, 2018, https://www.aboutamazon.com/news/workplace/how-a-door-became-a-desk-and-a-symbol-of-amazon.

license to practice law. I picked a strategic name for my new firm, and I had clients, thankfully, but I built everything else from that core.

Things look a little different for me now. But when you're starting out, the trick is to make it work and get the ball rolling. If you have partners, though, things get more complex—that's what we'll discuss in the next chapter.

3. STARTING A PARTNERSHIP

If you've decided a partnership might be right for you, you have a lot of planning to do. Before we dive into this section, let me address the critical difference between small partnerships and larger, more mature ones.

As a lawyer, you might be invited to join an existing partnership, which is very different from starting one from scratch. When you join an existing firm as a partner, the cake is already baked. You might get to add some frosting, but you're not going to fundamentally change the recipe. Starting from scratch gives you a chance to shape the vision and the culture, but it also means building everything from the ground up. It takes time and energy.

When I joined an existing partnership, everything was in place, and I plugged myself into the mix. There was no hassle, and all the business work—the partnership agreement, the legal entity, the office space, the staff—was already set up. Starting a new partnership is a completely different experience, and that's really what I'm discussing in this section.

Choosing a Partner

Years ago, two solo attorneys—Ellen the estate planning attorney and Stan the divorce lawyer—decided to leave their respective firms and create a partnership. They had been friends for a few years, and they figured their diverse practice areas would help, not hinder, their partnership. Feeling optimistic, they rented an office space, branded themselves as a boutique firm, and told each other that because of their disparate practice areas, they could easily offer each other referrals.

The referrals didn't materialize, and the two lawyers started bickering. Money wasn't coming in. Then Stan took a full three weeks off work for a long-awaited cruise with extended family.

Ellen was a workaholic pouring eighty hours a week into the firm; she felt like she was subsidizing someone else's lifestyle. Stan, meanwhile, felt micromanaged and misunderstood. The partnership ended with curt emails and a quiet scramble to separate websites and letterhead. The lesson? If the business isn't flowing before the partnership, don't expect a logo to change that.

These two went wrong right from the start. They picked the wrong partner.

I see this all the time. Plenty of lawyers who are friends decide to start a firm together, thinking it would be fun. The reality? That's an awful way to choose a partner. Just because you're great friends with someone doesn't necessarily mean you're going to be great business partners.

I've also seen people who decide on a partner because it makes sense on paper. *I do family law, and you do personal injury*, they think. *We can refer cases to each other, and it will work out.* That's not well thought out.

I often encounter lawyers with distinct, nonaligned practice areas who believe they'll grow by referring business to each other, like Ellen and Stan. This is usually wishful thinking. If you're not referring clients to each other before the partnership, you probably won't be able to once you're in a partnership either.

Choosing the right partner is paramount. If you're not on the same page, the chances of survival decrease significantly. Without alignment on core issues, friction is inevitable, even if you get along outside the office or courtroom.

I've consistently observed certain characteristics in enduring partnerships. Successful partners share common values and a common vision for the firm, trust each other, respect each other, treat each other fairly, and have a similar work ethic.

To maximize the partnership's potential, I recommend a thorough discussion of several high-level issues before agreeing to join forces. When evaluating a potential partnership, look for more than just complementary skills. You want strategically aligned practice areas, a team that can handle larger matters, and maybe even a broader geographic footprint. These are the things that create real momentum.

Think in terms of multipliers, not just additions. When choosing your business partner, I think a good rule of thumb is 1 + 1 = 3. The sum needs to be greater than any of the parts individually. Seek a combination of diverse skill sets, complementary and strategically aligned practice areas, a larger team for more important matters, or geographic expansion. And always aim for multipliers, not additions. The whole should be greater than the sum of its parts—in this case, you and the other attorney. If the partnership doesn't create a multiplier effect, it's probably more trouble than it's worth. You can never know for sure, but look for that potential. A good partnership should amplify what each of you brings to the table. If it doesn't, the partnership might end up being more of a burden than a benefit.

That said, there are exceptions. You can find a list of questions to explore with your potential partner here: https://www.lawfirmgc.com/life-cycle-resources/. It's free, and you can use it for discussion with your potential partner to ensure a good match before you start pouring time and money into your joint venture.

Partnership Agreements

Law firms are different from other businesses. We are governed by strict regulations and ethics rules and opinions. Other businesses can get away with shenanigans that we can't. We can't lock attorneys down with noncompete agreements, and we can't force clients to stay with us. Law firm breakup issues can be different from those of other business dissolutions, so an off-the-shelf partnership agreement typically won't work. In fact, I've seen instances where it was counterproductive.

A good law firm partnership agreement is like a marriage contract and a prenup for your law firm. Establishing a partnership agreement isn't a formality; it is the foundation of the firm's internal governance and must address all aspects of the relationship. Issues such as decision-making, equity owner compensation, and exit scenarios need to be clearly outlined from the start.

It's easy to wonder if this is necessary. You get along with your partner so well that you have no doubt you can resolve disagreements amicably. You're not alone in believing this. I've come across long-term law partners who have operated on a handshake. I commend them for making it work, but I don't recommend that approach. In my experience, it works until it doesn't. And when it doesn't, things can get very expensive very quickly.

Like marriages, law firm partnerships can fall apart over time. People change, situations change, visions change. Life happens, and it's better to address this potentiality on the front end when everyone gets along.

Every law firm needs a thoroughly written partnership agreement that lays out everyone's rights and obligations in a variety of scenarios. This should not be controversial. If you don't have a written (and signed!) agreement, get one in place as soon as possible. Even among lawyers, it's surprisingly common for agreements to go unsigned despite being drafted. I've seen it, and more than once. Such an oversight can undo years of collaboration in a matter of weeks.

Simply put, you need to draft the agreement, sign it, and stick to it. Creating clarity from the beginning prevents confusion and conflict down the road. That investment now could save you time and money in the future. As you likely tell your own clients, "It's cheaper to do it now than later."

Also, partnerships aren't a good DIY task. I don't recommend you draft your partnership agreement by yourself. I draft a lot of law firm partnership agreements, and I also handle a lot of law firm breakups. I've found that doing each really helps the other because every time I handle a breakup, I see new issues or arguments. Those get addressed in my next partnership agreement.

When I draft partnership agreements, my lawyer clients often ask new questions and give new insights. This improves my agreements time after time. I also review a lot of partnership agreements drafted by others. If I see a good provision, I will incorporate it into my agreements.

When it comes to structuring a law firm, the structure you choose can depend on a number of factors. One factor to consider is how many partners you have. If you have a lot of partners, you may want to choose one structure over another. It may be that one partner is the founder, more senior, or a more dominant player in the firm and, because of that, should have a more substantial role in decision-making.

With that in mind, let's discuss the areas this partnership agreement should cover.

Decision-Making

Decision-making within a partnership is a critical area requiring thoughtful design. That's because, without a good plan in place, this is one of the most contentious areas that can lead to nastiness and law firm breakups. By understanding what questions your plan needs to address, considering common decision-making structures, and avoiding the popular but inadvisable consensus approach, you can set your law firm up for seamless and conflict-free decision-making for years to come.

Questions Your Decision-Making Plan Should Address

When creating your governance structure, here some questions to consider:

- In a fifty-fifty structure, what happens when there's a disagreement?
- How will you resolve deadlocks?
- Should all partners share all firm responsibilities equally?
- Should defined responsibilities be assigned to certain partners or positions?
- Is unanimous, supermajority, or majority consent required for decisions?

- Are voting rights proportional to ownership percentage?
- Should major decisions be distinguished from minor decisions?
- What procedures control deadlock situations?

Three Decision-Making Structures to Consider

Every law firm has a different optimal decision-making structure. Some firms opt for an uneven voting split, such as sixty–forty. Others may have equal voting rights with a deadlock provision in their agreement.

A firm's governance form can vary depending on the firm's size and complexity, but the essential point remains: Rules and roles should be defined early and clearly. Without them, confusion and conflict are almost guaranteed. Consider these three scenarios:

Scenario 1: The managing partner. A single, recognized leader that everyone knows is the decision-maker. Maybe it's an older, more established lawyer with the larger book of business partnering with a young up-and-comer who is not yet on equal footing.

Scenario 2: The executive committee. A smaller group of people within the partnership that gets to drive decisions. Even within that executive committee setup, you would likely designate a managing partner to take care of day-to-day operations.

Scenario 3: The collective. All the partners get to vote on everything. A lot of people call it governing by consensus.

What works for one firm will not necessarily work for another, so you must choose the right setup that fits your facts.

Why Consensus Rarely Works

A word of caution: Lawyers, by default, tend to have an opinion on everything—even when we shouldn't. Sometimes we have no knowledge or context to form a valid, carefully considered opinion. Still, we like to say what we think. We often come in with a forceful opinion and don't care much about the consequences. We want to be heard, but that bogs everything down, and it's a habit worth breaking.

A lot of law firm partners say, "Oh, we make all our decisions by consensus." I think that's a mistake. I've seen it from the inside more than once, and I've seen it with my clients too. When decisions are made by consensus, particularly in a firm with many partners, one of three things usually happens: no decision is ever made, any decisions get so watered down that they become meaningless, or decision-making takes forever. It drags on, and you lose your competitive edge.

Therefore, consensus decision-making is a mistake in any firm. I recommend you delegate to a strong managing partner or to a small committee.

Closely related to consensus is the demand for full democracy, which some firms think they want. That's fine as long as the voting requirements aren't too high. Some decisions could be made by majority vote, others by supermajority. You can define those rules. But again, while it can work early on, consensus is not a way to sustainably govern or succeed in the long term.

Exit Scenarios

Nearly every partnership agreement needs to address exit scenarios. An exit from a firm is nearly always stressful, and having a plan in place helps to mitigate contention and give you a plan of action. A well-drafted agreement addresses what happens when a partner leaves, no matter the reason.

When is notice to the firm required? How are clients given notice? What payments or buyouts will the firm make to the departing attorney? There is a lot to consider here, and it's best to be as detailed as possible.

Your payment/buyout plan often depends on the size and type of firm, and these plans can differ depending on how a partner exits. A lawyer who is kicked out for bad behavior (like stealing from trust funds) shouldn't get paid the same as a lawyer who is retiring.

These are the categories every agreement should deal with. I usually think of them as "friendly exits," which have nothing to do with conflict, and "unfriendly exits," which are far more contentious.

Friendly Exits

When a partner has a "friendly exit," there are typically little to no disputes. Everyone is still getting along. There are three scenarios that I view as "friendly" exits: death, disability or incapacity, and retirement.

Death: No one wants to think about it, but death comes for us all, and it should be addressed in the partnership agreement. At one of my previous firms, one of the partners died within six months of my joining. Luckily, the partnership agreement had a provision dealing with this, and we had six partners and many others to assist in the transition of clients and cases.

Disability or incapacity: What happens if one of the partners becomes disabled or incapacitated? Whether through accident, illness, or something else, it's best to have a plan if someone needs to bow out.

Retirement: Is there an age requirement? Is there a buyout or retirement payments? Does the retiring partner get to stay on with the firm in a different capacity?

Unfriendly Exits

Unfriendly exits, unlike friendly exits, can lead to serious disputes. I highly recommend you plan for them in your partnership agreement. If you don't, things could get very ugly, very fast.

One unfriendly exit is voluntary departure to practice elsewhere. When an attorney voluntarily leaves, they often take cases or staff along with them. This can cause a lot of stress and angst on both sides. You can't stop someone from leaving, but your agreement can address what happens when someone leaves. If your agreement doesn't comprehensively cover this, it's a recipe for a huge fight.

Another unfriendly exit is expulsion. There can be expulsion for cause or without cause. Either way, a partner gets kicked out of the firm. Typically, when you're in a sizable partnership, you need to address expulsion. But expulsion isn't appropriate in every scenario or partnership. In an equal two-person partnership, for example, how can one partner kick the other out?

I want to talk more about expulsion because, unlike the other exit scenarios, this can go a variety of ways. You can do it for cause, which, in agreements, I call the "bad boy or girl provision." So if you're stealing from the firm, you get disbarred, or you commit a felony, you can get kicked out of a firm for cause. In your partnership agreement, you can lay out behaviors that can result in expulsion and what the expulsion process looks like.

But sometimes it's just not working out. Differences in personality or work ethic can result in someone being ousted from the partnership without cause. You didn't necessarily do anything wrong—the partners just weren't working well together.

Generally speaking, expulsion is used when there are more than two partners. But there are exceptions. Let's say you've got a dominant leader and their partner holds a small minority stake. In such cases, expulsion of the minority partner might be possible. But what happens in a fifty-fifty partnership? Who retains control? There are procedures for handling such situations, and we can discuss them if they apply to your firm.

Last, let's touch on dissolution. In certain circumstances, a firm can continue to exist when one lawyer leaves. But when a firm dissolves, the firm itself is over. Dissolution can happen in combination with any other exit scenarios or on its own. This means the end of not only the partnership, but also the firm itself.

Compensation Agreements within a Partnership

Then, there's partner compensation. Rather than including this in your partnership agreement, I suggest you make this a separate agreement referenced in but not embedded within the partnership agreement.

Why? A separate agreement gives you more flexibility to make changes, and compensation models often need to evolve over time. As a firm grows, partners take on new roles and market conditions shift, so the compensation system should adapt. Having the space to revise the compensation terms without reopening broader negotiations over the firm's entire partnership agreement makes this process much easier.

That said, revisions should be infrequent—no more than annually, and preferably every two to three years at most. And never change a compensation plan midyear. Doing so undermines trust and morale.

I have yet to see the perfect law firm compensation model, and I doubt one exists. I have, however, assisted many new partnerships in creating fair, dynamic law firm compensation models. Let's talk about what you need to include and how you can structure your compensation model to work well for your firm.

Compensation Models

As an initial proposition, remember that incentives often drive behavior. Compensation systems create incentives, and lawyers will always work the formula. That includes you and your business partners. That's why, when you create your compensation system, you should think about both short-term and long-term behaviors you want to encourage in yourself and your partner.

If you want to increase the chances of a successful transition, you have to think about the long-term effects of your compensation system. This is where many lawyers go awry. So if you only incentivize origination and production, partners will only focus on origination and production. Other important components to prolonged firm success, such as training, mentorship, operations, team building, and knowledge management, will suffer because they aren't compensated in the same way.

After working on countless compensation agreements, I've come to the conclusion that eat-what-you-kill compensation systems of all varieties have an extended adverse effect on the firm life cycle. They might appear good in the short term, but eventually they become counterproductive. They tend to encourage silos, discourage teamwork, and lead to a loose confederation of "mini–law firms" within a partnership. They make succession planning more difficult.

On the other hand, compensation solely based on ownership percentage can become unfair. The partners' situations may change over time, including their work ethic and ability to bring in work. There is a potential freeloader problem that can lead to resentments.

Here's my current thinking on partnership compensation. A significant portion of an equity partner's compensation can (and probably should) be based on some measurable production goals. But there should also be a meaningful portion based purely on equity ownership. Otherwise, how does an equity partner candidate adequately measure their return on investment with the firm? Using a combination of these two approaches creates a rising-tide effect while tempering the freeloader issue.

Adding a discretionary component is also advisable. It allows the firm to account for circumstances that don't fit neatly into metrics—maternity leave, health issues, or contributions like implementing a new technology system. This flexibility promotes fairness and cohesion among partners.

As an example, say we have two experienced attorneys, Kyle and Florence, who each contribute $25,000 in capital to get their new firm off the ground. They agreed to 60 percent performance-based compensation, but they expanded "performance" to include mentoring junior attorneys, developing internal systems, leading hiring efforts, and building out knowledge management tools.

During the years that followed, this paid off. In their third year, Florence spent months creating a training curriculum for new associates, and Kyle led the charge on implementing a firm-wide customer relationship management base and knowledge base. These weren't billable hours, but they were foundational to the firm's long-term success.

The remaining 40 percent of Ellen and Kyle's compensation came from profit distributions tied strictly to equity ownership. That portion constituted a return on investment for the two partners, making them feel like their risk was paying off.

I hope you can see why I think the best approach is typically a hybrid system. A portion of a partner's compensation should reflect performance, client development, and file work. Another portion should reflect equity ownership, as this ensures that those who built the firm continue to benefit from its success. It also facilitates smoother transitions in leadership and ownership over time.

Your Brand-New Law Firm

There's no substitute for careful planning when launching a law firm. Whether going solo or partnering with others, the choices made in the early stages lay the foundation for everything that follows. Taking the time to set expectations, create written agreements, and design adaptable systems is a must.

Law firm partnerships, in particular, demand foresight, communication, and a willingness to evolve because of the added complexity of two leaders. Those who succeed in building strong, lasting firms are thoughtful businesspeople who understand the importance of structure, trust, and shared purpose.

When I first set out on my own, I thought passion and grit would be enough. And while they helped, I quickly learned that building a practice takes more than mere determination. At a bare minimum, you need to know three things:

1. How to get clients
2. How to manage clients
3. How to run client matters

If you don't already have those down, start there. Study them. Practice them. Learn them fast. They're the pillars everything else rests on.

Whether you're taking these steps alone or with a partner, this is no time to rush forward without thinking. Take the time, have the serious brainstorm sessions, and do the work on the front end. You'll either lay the foundation and increase the chances for success or find out that the partnership is not right for you.

Those first few months? They'll probably be the busiest of your life. You'll be juggling business setup, marketing, and client work—sometimes all at once. It's easy to feel overwhelmed.

I know there's a lot to think about, and it's easy to make mistakes or miss critical details. Trust me when I say it gets easier. Many things that seem overwhelming at the beginning—setting up your tax ID, opening your business bank account, launching your website, figuring out email systems, even the small stuff like buying a stapler—only happen once. The storm settles, the waves calm, and things get more manageable. So hang in there.

4. GROWTH PART I—CLIENTS

When I started Law Firm GC in February 2018, I was running a fully virtual lifestyle firm. I was the only one working there, and it wasn't a full-time gig. It took a while to get off the ground because of my involvement with Tim's company and because I wasn't actively trying to grow it.

I hit capacity, so I hired a contract attorney to help me. Then we hit capacity, so I added another. Then we hit capacity *again*.

That's when I hit the proverbial fork in the road. I had to decide: Do I want to grow my firm, or do I want to keep it at its current size and start turning work away?

I was mulling this over at the gym one day in 2022, sitting on a bench, half listening to a podcast about business growth and goals. Suddenly, a thought hit me hard. *If I don't give this a real shot—if I don't try to grow this firm—I'm going to regret it on my deathbed.*

And a second thought came right after: *If someone else builds the firm I could have built, I'm going to be pissed.*

I made the decision that morning: I was going to go for it and grow Law Firm GC as much as possible. I've been on that road ever since. At the time of writing, we've got six attorneys and three non-attorney team members, and we're still growing.

How did I do it? In this chapter, I'll explain a big part of how with the second stage of the law firm life cycle. We'll start by looking outward at marketing, because no matter what kind of law you practice, getting that ball rolling is pivotal. Your firm has to be able to get clients, and that means marketing. We will also look at some risks that can arise when growing your client base.

I'm not a marketing consultant or coach. There are plenty of marketing experts—people you can follow, hire, or learn from to help you market your firm. But I do want to talk about marketing here because there are special marketing considerations for lawyers. Whether it's building your marketing stack, garnering referrals and leads, or managing social media and advertising, you always need to toe the line and avoid doing anything that could land you in trouble with the bar.

The Law Firm Marketing Stack

For a lot of lawyers, marketing feels overwhelming. I get it. I've felt it, too, and if I'm being honest, I still do. You look around and see other lawyers—my friends like Tim

Semelroth, Tom Spiggle, or Christopher Earley—putting out high-level content, building real visibility. It makes you think, *If I could do half of what they're doing, I could really scale this thing. I had better get moving.* Here's just some of what these and other mature, large firms cover:

- Referrals
- Speaking
- Writing
- Social media
- Email
- Print mailers
- Search engine optimization
- Advertising

That's a lot you can do to market yourself and your firm, and trying to make it all happen as soon as you open your doors leads straight to overwhelm. That, in turn, often leads to inaction.

Here's what I suggest and what I did myself: Don't do everything at once. If you try that, you will stretch yourself too thin. Instead, build your marketing stack one channel at a time. Choose one approach, focus on it, and get good at it. (If I had to choose one, it would be developing referral relationships.) Once that's running smoothly, you can move on to the next until you have a multifaceted and effective marketing stack.

Here's what I chose to start doing year by year. It might not be right for your firm, but it worked for me:

- 2008—Focused on referrals (This is a long game; more on that in a second.)
- 2010—Sent weekly emails to clients and referral sources
- 2011—Spoke and wrote to lawyers on issues in my niche practice
- 2018—Started Law Firm GC (Notice I started building a network before I started the business.)
- 2022—Posted on LinkedIn regularly
- 2023—Launched the *Founding Partner Podcast* (Check it out!)
- 2024—Started a monthly print newsletter (Direct message me on LinkedIn if you want to be on the list.)
- 2025—Wrote this book

When I started approaching marketing this way, everything changed. I built routines, saw what worked, and stopped getting pulled in five directions at once. And yes, I still do plenty of other things to market my business, but I couldn't start by trying to make it all happen instantaneously. If I had stuck with that approach, I probably would have burned out—or never started at all.

Marketing as an Ecosystem and the Importance of Consistency

As you can see, there's a lot involved in a law firm marketing stack. There's also no single path to implementing some or all of it. Not every law firm can use every one of these components in their marketing strategy. Some of these tactics take longer to implement than others. But if you stick with it, you'll find the marketing stack components that fit your firm.

Just as our law firms have a life cycle, they reside inside an ecosystem. Think of your business development as seeking food in your habitat—what decisions can you make? There isn't one right way to do this. You can farm, you can hunt, you can set traps, you can gather.

In marketing, speaking works. Writing works. Search engine optimization, social media, paid ads, networking—they all work. I know lawyers who have built seven-figure practices using only one of these channels.

A critical part of this is consistency. You can't go hunting once and eat for the rest of your life. Likewise, sporadic business development won't move the needle. The magic happens when you show up consistently over a long period of time. Your efforts compound, momentum builds, and the results start to feel exponential. We're all busy, but it's worth taking the time to check this box every day, even if it's a small step.

Established firms that have been around for years usually include most of what I listed above in their marketing strategy. It's easy to look at that and think, *There's no way I'll ever catch up*. So don't try. Start with one thing. Do it well. Do it long enough to get results. Then add another. Stack slowly and intentionally.

That's when the magic happens, and everything starts to compound. Your podcast drives traffic to your site. Your posts strengthen your brand. Your newsletter builds trust. Your YouTube videos close the loop. The trees you planted years ago start to bear fruit. Each part of the ecosystem supports the others, and the combined effect is bigger than the sum of its parts. Soon you'll have a feast on your table.

Referrals and Leads

It's not always going to work the same way for everyone, but the tried-and-true approach for any law practice is to start with referral marketing. But there are many restrictions and considerations when it comes to referrals and leads for law firms that you'll need to keep in mind as you pursue referrals and leads.

The Basics of Developing Referral Relationships

The most reliable and affordable approach (especially early on) is to build referral relationships. That means connecting with other lawyers or professionals who are likely to refer clients to you. Build relationships and develop referral channels—that's the foundation.

The other notable thing I always recommend for anyone starting a firm is to begin with two lists: a list of referral sources and a list of clients and former clients. Then figure out a way to stay in touch with these people. That could be through emails, print mailings, phone calls, coffee meetings, birthday cards—whatever you can do consistently.

No Paying Non lawyers for Leads

Once you start fostering referral relationships, there are right ways and wrong ways to go about getting more referrals. And by "wrong," I don't just mean ineffective—I mean unethical.

Most lawyers understand that you're not supposed to share fees with nonlawyers, even if they refer cases to you. This prohibition used to be universal across the country, but things are changing. Leading that change is the state of Arizona, which now allows law firms to have non-lawyer owners, and those owners can naturally profit from the business. Arizona has also eliminated the prohibition on sharing legal fees with nonlawyers. But Arizona is the exception, not the norm.

In most jurisdictions, you can't pay non lawyers commissions for specific leads. In other words, if a non lawyer refers you a case, you can't pay them for it. That's the rule, and you need to follow it when working with third parties outside your firm. Another question that comes up a lot is, Can I share fees with my *internal* staff?

Many jurisdictions do allow profit sharing with employees. That said, there is a right way and a wrong way to do it. So check your jurisdiction's rules. As a general proposition, you can't bonus a nonlawyer employee for bringing in a specific case. If an employee refers their neighbor to the firm, you can't give them a referral fee. Instead, you must create a bonus plan based on the overall firm profits.

Referral Fees to Other Lawyers

Unlike referral fees to non lawyers, referral fees to lawyers are often allowed, under specific circumstances. Again, the first factor is your location. Every state is different, so first and foremost, check your local jurisdiction's rules. Some states are more permissive when it comes to referral fees between lawyers, while others prohibit them or put limits on how much can be paid.

California is relatively permissive—it allows referral fees between lawyers even if they don't share responsibility for the case as long as the client consents in writing. Florida, on the other hand, requires joint responsibility and caps the referral fee, often at 25 percent if the case is referred before a lawsuit is filed. New York allows fee sharing, too, but only if the referring lawyer either does some of the work or agrees to take joint responsibility. Again, the client must be informed and agree in writing in these cases.

As you can see, even if your jurisdiction allows referral fees, that doesn't mean you're free to handle them however you want. You still have to do it the right way, the ethical way. That means complying with the specific requirements in your state's rules of professional conduct. You don't want to find yourself on the wrong side of an ethics complaint because you skipped a step or assumed something was okay without proper research.

Referral Fees on Contingency Cases Versus Hourly Cases

It's virtually impossible to ethically pay an attorney a referral fee on an hourly matter. Generally, referral fee rules require that the referring lawyer has contributed to the case in some way. If you're not billing hours on the matter and you're not in the same firm, it's hard to justify getting paid a piece of the fee.

Most ethics rules are written in a way that makes it extremely difficult to structure an hourly referral to be both ethical and practical. You can't say "Since you charge four hundred dollars an hour, I'll take fifty dollars of that" and have that pass muster. Plus, frankly, it's not economically feasible for an hourly lawyer to pay out a referral fee on that basis from an operational and overhead standpoint.

Because of this, referral fees tend to work best in contingency-type cases. Let's say I get a trucking case, but I don't practice that type of law. Instead, I refer the case to a truck wreck lawyer. I can do enough on that case—screen it, communicate with the client, maybe assist in the handoff or stay involved in some way—to justify a percentage payment of the eventual fee. This is an ethical way to handle a lawyer referral payment.

Advertising

Advertising encompasses many channels: billboards, radio, TV, even park benches. For the most part, these ads tend to pass ethical muster. But then there's digital advertising: social media ads, Google Ads, and anything else online. Lawyers can get into trouble with internet and social media ads, especially when they've hired someone else to run them—someone who doesn't specialize in legal marketing and doesn't understand or care about the ethical rules governing what you can and can't say.

Social Media Restrictions for Law Firms

Social media marketing is all the rage, and for good reason. Without much cost, you can get your name out there and generate cases and clients from social media, whether it's from actual advertising or more indirect methods like posting. In either case, you must be careful to follow the ethics rules.

Just like with other forms of marketing, it's smart to look at state-specific ethics opinions. Many states have published ethics opinions on what can and can't be done on social media. For instance, New York has cautioned lawyers against posting even vague case details online, as doing so could inadvertently reveal confidential client information.

In Texas, in some circumstances, social media posts may be considered advertising and must comply with all applicable advertising rules, including disclaimers and recordkeeping. Meanwhile, California stipulates that endorsements or testimonials on platforms like LinkedIn must not be misleading and should clearly state whether the endorser is a client or peer. Familiarizing yourself with these location-specific guidelines beforehand can save you a lot of trouble later.

In general, attorneys are prohibited from using comparative language in any advertising materials, including online content, throughout the United States. This concept applies broadly to all law firm advertising. Most attorneys know better than to state something like, "We're the best lawyers in town" or "We're better than the competitor down the street."

If you flout the rules, the consequences can be severe, including a bar complaint. Most often, the state bar will issue a warning and instruct you to stop, but that alone puts you at risk. In some cases, you may receive a formal reprimand that becomes part of your professional record. And if the violation is particularly serious, the disciplinary outcome could go as far as suspension or disbarment. To avoid this unfortunate prospect, check your rules—or check with an attorney who is familiar with them.

The Dangers of Outsourcing Advertising

The rapid evolution of digital marketing has introduced new risks, particularly when attorneys hire non-legal marketing agencies. While billboard and radio advertisements are fairly straightforward, some online strategies—especially those involving lead generation—are extremely aggressive and far more likely to violate ethical rules.

I recently saw an ad on social media filled with false and misleading statements that included a promise of a payout on a car wreck claim in weeks. There was another that said, "Know someone who has been injured in an accident? Refer a case today and earn five hundred dollars." I hope all lawyers know that they're not allowed to run an advertisement like this one. But does the marketing firm that ran that ad know about this restriction? Do they even care?

If a law firm is behind this ad or is the recipient of leads from this ad, does that put their lawyers' licenses at risk? I wouldn't want to run that risk. From a bar regulator's perspective, it probably doesn't matter that the law firm didn't run that ad directly. When attorneys outsource marketing to third parties who engage in unethical practices, the attorneys *themselves* can be held accountable. This includes being liable for the misconduct of any vendors or marketers you hire.

As you might imagine, this can get ugly. I've seen examples of Google Ads purchases that clearly violated the law. One of these involved a marketing company I'll call Blunder Marketing and a large firm I'll call Firm Q.

Blunder Marketing had law firm clients (though not Firm Q) for whom they bought Google AdWords advertisements. These ads were triggered when users searched "Firm Q." In the paid search results, the law firm appeared with Firm Q's name explicitly listed in their ad. But when potential clients clicked the ad, they were directed to a different firm's intake department.

Firm Q wasn't happy about this, and they hired me to help. After receiving a cease and desist letter from me, that law firm claimed it had no knowledge of the breach and assured me that it would never happen again. We've been watching, and so far we haven't seen anything. But if it happens again, we will be filing a lawsuit instead of sending a letter.

Regardless of intent, this isn't a situation you want to be in as a law firm. If the marketing company you hired uses black hat unethical approaches, it could get you in trouble with the bar. If you're lucky, you'll just get sued. If you're unlucky, you might be out of a job.

How to Hire Marketing Companies

Given all that, how can you find a trustworthy advertising company? You may think a marketing agency that specializes in lawyers might do a better job and be more familiar with the restrictions on legal advertising, but that's not always the case. Even among those companies, unethical players abound. For instance, the marketing agency improperly using Firm Q's name worked with many law firms.

About a month ago, one of my employees ran an internet search for one of our clients. Up popped an ad for a competing law firm—with our client's name right in the ad. That's illegal, and after we sent a letter, they apologized profusely and removed the ad. You don't want to put yourself in that situation.

If you decide to use a law firm marketing agency, do your homework. Don't go with the first one you find. Spend some time identifying an agency that seems trustworthy—one with great reviews, a strong track record, and a stellar reputation. And once you find such an agency, don't go on autopilot. As they work, ask them to show you what they're doing, and do your own research to ensure that they're being honest about the campaigns they're running.

A marketing agency may tell you they're taking one approach, but since your law license is on the line, it doesn't hurt to do your own research. There are ways to independently research and confirm that a marketing firm is delivering on their promises. Having someone on your team take this extra step can save you from potential litigation later on.

Special Rules for Traditional Mass Media Advertisements

If you choose to incorporate traditional mass media advertisements into your strategy, it's once again time to look into your jurisdiction's ethics rules. Some states require specific disclosures depending on the type of advertising. Florida requires that many types of advertisements, including direct mail, be submitted to the state bar for review at least twenty days before they're sent out. They also must be clearly marked as advertisements. Meanwhile, Texas mandates that ads include the name of at least one attorney responsible for the content along with the principal office location.

The rules vary from state to state, so you have to check. Also, most states require you to retain copies of all your advertising materials for a certain period of time. Think of your ads like tax records: You may need to keep them for three to five years depending on your jurisdiction. The bottom line is that if you're going to go down the mass media route, you must make sure your ads pass ethical muster.

Grow Your Client Base, Grow Your Firm

To grow your firm, you have to grow your client base. For me, that meant doing a lot of legwork years before starting my firm—fostering relationships with other attorneys and clients, keeping lists, and even sending out handwritten birthday cards. For many other firms, it means paying for advertising online or elsewhere.

Whether you use referrals, advertising, or both to grow your business, remember to respect the letter of the law. You don't want to run into trouble, so grow your firm ethically and legally, and when word gets out, you'll have more clients than you know what to do with.

5. GROWTH PART II—
RECRUITING AND HIRING

Your vision may be to keep your firm small. Or perhaps you want to expand. Or maybe you would like to become a regional or national operation with multiple locations. Whatever scale you're looking for, a new firm needs traction to survive. Work starts to roll in, and eventually, you and your partners can't handle everything by yourselves. There's client work, and there's business work: invoicing, bookkeeping, marketing, website, and administrative work. The list goes on and on.

As the legal work grows, the ability for attorneys to handle everything else diminishes. Honestly, you shouldn't be doing most of that administrative work anyway; you need to bring in help. Maybe it starts with outsourcing certain functions, like bookkeeping. Maybe it's bringing on a virtual assistant. Maybe you need to add another attorney.

Eventually, this leads to scaling. The firm starts to grow from the foundation that has been built: more staff, more attorneys, and potentially more locations. Along with that comes more complexity, more challenges, and more issues. I've been through some of that, and I guide my clients through it all the time.

My point, really, is this: If you want to grow your law firm, you can't just keep taking on more work; you have to hire people to do the work. There's no way around it. This includes hiring other attorneys and non-attorney support staff, like administrative assistants, bookkeepers, and the like. With both types of staff, attorney and non-attorney, you'll need to think about everything from types of employees to conflicts analysis to onboarding. This is the second part of the growth phase of the life cycle of a law firm: internal growth.

Hiring Lawyers

Once there's more legal work coming into your firm than you can personally handle, it's time to bring in another attorney. There are many ways a law firm can grow its legal team; you're not limited to only hiring full-time associates. You can—and often should—explore different structures depending on your needs, risk tolerance, and strategic goals. Each path comes with its own set of pros and cons, so let's explore those here.

Full-Time W-2 Employees

Full-time W-2 employees are the traditional route. When you hire a full-time W-2 attorney, you're committing to payroll, benefits, overhead—all of it. Whether they have work or not, you're paying these attorneys. It's a considerable financial commitment, but it also gives you the most control over their time and output. You may want to go this route once your firm has enough work to fully justify the investment, but it might not be the first type of attorney hire you make.

Contract Attorneys

A contract attorney works on a project-by-project basis. You pay them only when they work, and their ties to your firm aren't as strong as those of an "of counsel" attorney.

This arrangement is ideal if you're swamped this month but unsure about next month; if you need help with document review, motion drafting, or discovery on a specific matter; and if you want to test a potential long-term hire without commitment.

If the work slows down, the contract ends. No payroll, no benefits, no long-term obligation.

Of Counsel

Of counsel attorneys are different from contract attorneys, though sometimes the terms get used loosely. The "of counsel" arrangement is often more of a commitment than that with a contract attorney, and the structure gives both the firm and the attorney more flexibility than the traditional full-time attorney arrangement. Typically, this arrangement means the lawyer isn't a full-time employee but has a close relationship with the firm. You can agree on a pay structure that reduces your financial exposure. It's a flexible, scalable way to grow without the full weight of a permanent hire.

The of counsel model works well for many different scenarios:

- An older attorney who wants to slow down but stay involved
- A parent or caregiver who doesn't want to work full time
- A solo practitioner who doesn't have enough of their own work to stay busy
- An attorney with a complementary practice area that expands your firm's offerings
- A newer law firm that can't yet afford another full-time attorney but needs some extra help

Once you've figured out how you want to structure the relationship, the next step is the hiring process. And a critical part of that process—regardless of which structure you choose—is the conflict check.

Conflicts Analysis

You can bring on attorneys straight out of law school, which may help you avoid some conflicts issues. But many firms grow by hiring laterally—lawyers who are already practicing at other firms. There's a process to lateral hiring, and one noteworthy issue is conflicts analysis.

At some stage in the hiring process, you must conduct a thorough conflict check for new attorneys. It's not optional. In most, if not all, jurisdictions, if one attorney has an actual conflict of interest, it will be imputed to the entire law firm, subjecting the firm to disqualification. This is why a conflict check is of utmost importance when bringing in a new lateral hire. This step protects your clients, your firm, and your bar license.

Here are some common conflicts that may arise:

Direct conflicts: Let's say you're litigating against another lawyer—opposing counsel on an active matter—and then you invite them to join your firm. That's a conflict, as they would be switching sides mid-case.

Imputed conflicts: Imputed conflicts are trickier. Suppose the lawyer you're hiring didn't work directly on a matter that's adverse to your firm, but their firm is involved. Even if that specific lawyer had no direct contact with the case, conflicts can still be imputed to them—and by extension, to your firm.

Cross-client conflicts: Let's say the lawyer you're hiring is bringing over five cases. If one of those involves a party your firm represents in a different matter, even if the two lawsuits are unrelated, it still creates a conflict.

Cross-client conflicts can get really messy. Let's say that at Firm 1, A is suing B. At your firm (Firm 2), B is suing C. If the new lawyer tries to bring that A v. B case with them, it could create an irreconcilable conflict if you already represent B in any capacity.

There are ways to address this, such as declining to bring certain matters over or withdrawing from conflicting cases. But you may have to pass on the hire entirely—at least until the cases are over. Screening lawyers is typically not a viable solution.

Non lawyer Lateral Conflicts

Even non lawyers can create a conflict imputed to an entire law firm, causing disqualification in certain cases. For instance, a paralegal who worked on a case at another firm can bring confidential knowledge to their new employer. If the new law firm represents the adverse party and inadvertently assigns that paralegal to the case, that's a conflict. If you don't handle it correctly, a move like that will likely get your firm disqualified and force you to withdraw.

That said, you don't necessarily have to pass on a non-attorney hire if they have worked at a law firm with a conflict of interest. Make sure your jurisdiction allows screening and that the appropriate and timely screening measures have been implemented. The specific screening measures differ depending on the circumstances, but there are many keys to successful screening:

- Implementing the screening as soon as practical after a firm knows (or reasonably should know) it is needed
- Giving appropriate instruction to everyone about the obligation not to disclose information related to the representation
- Isolating the non lawyer from any participation in the matter
- Instituting procedures to prevent the non lawyer from accessing files regarding the matter

Culture, Values, and Wellness

Law firm culture was once ignored, but it has gained a lot of attention in recent years. The old mindset was simple: show up, work hard, endure the stress, and don't expect much concern for your personal life or well-being. Toxic environments, long hours, and a lack of support were the norm.

But that's changing. Whether you're doing it intentionally or not, your firm has a culture. The question is whether you're shaping it by design or letting it develop by default. More and more law firm owners and leaders are beginning to understand the importance of creating a healthy, positive culture.

A strong firm culture isn't just the right thing to do; it also helps you as the business owner, as it is both a recruitment tool and a retention strategy. Law firm owners often tell me that they can't find the right people. It's true that good talent is hard to find—and even harder to keep.

Podcast Feature: Tom Tona and Kevin McManus on Culture

On *Founding Partner Podcast*, I've interviewed several law firm owners who strongly emphasize culture. Two of these owners are featured in this section: Tom Tona and Kevin McManus.

Tom Tona, the owner of TonaLaw, is based in New York and runs a successful personal injury and no-fault collection firm. Kevin McManus runs McManus and McManus Attorneys at Law, with offices in Kansas and Missouri. Both lawyers say their success has to do with a healthy company culture, and both identified several key aspects of their approach.

The Onus Is on the Owner

Tom has a lot of great ideas about culture, starting with culture as the owner's responsibility. "My job is making sure that my culture scales with my business," he told me. "I don't want a business that makes a lot of money but turns toxic, right?" Kevin had something similar to say: "I kind of think of myself as director of culture and director of values, along with other things."

Tom in particular takes huge personal responsibility for positive culture in the workplace because of his upbringing. "I was bullied as a kid," he told me. "I'm five foot seven and weighed one hundred and twenty-five pounds when I graduated high school, and I had the mouth on me that I have now. So I got beat up a lot. I got into martial arts because of it." Tom, who now has a black belt in jujitsu, takes culture seriously. "If I see somebody bullying in my office or I see somebody talking escalatingly rough in my office, I'm the guy that leaves the desk and goes and talks to them."

Hire the Right People

Kevin places a lot of emphasis on the hiring process, screening for personality through multiple rounds so those bullies never make it past the door. "It doesn't matter how great a litigator you are," he said. "If you're a complete jerk, we just won't work well together. You'll cause more problems in our firm than it's worth. Many of your listeners probably have been at firms where they have someone who's productive and good at their job, so to speak, but terrible with people and a real cancer on the culture in the firm. And it's not worth it."

Tom also believes that culture starts with the right people. "You gotta hand-select the people you want on that bullet train to succeed with you," he explained. "You gotta make sure you're all in the same alignment, in the vision, the values, all that stuff." Part of this is finding the right second-in-command; for Tom, it's his integrator, Jamira. "Two people, one brain," he said. "It's got to be someone who's executing on your vision."

Culture Across Borders

Kevin's firm includes international employees, so he has to take extra care to foster a positive company culture. Part of this means an integrated virtual meeting system so everyone can participate, but Kevin also goes the extra mile to include his virtual employees in the perks of the job. When his firm developed a new client gift package, for example, he wanted his employees to partake as well. "We shipped them all over the world," he said. "We sent one to every single one of our VAs. We paid all the tariffs and everything."

Kevin has even found a way to invite his international team to holiday parties. "We've done a holiday dinner where we rented out a room in a local restaurant and got a big screen in there," he told me. "We had all of our people from throughout the world eating with us, and we paid for their meals."

Retention

Hiring is hard. Watching attorneys walk away with your clients is maybe harder. The obvious fix isn't trying to stop them from leaving, or trapping them with restrictive covenants. But you can create an environment people don't want to leave in the first place.

Build a firm that attorneys are proud to be part of. Foster a culture that makes people stay for reasons beyond a paycheck. Give your team real opportunities to grow. When you create a firm culture that people enjoy, the word spreads.

A healthy company culture helps attract new talent, and it also helps you keep the great people you already have. Retention is just as important—if not more important—than recruitment.

A huge part of this relies on your leadership skills, and for many new law firm owners, this is a brand-new skill. One aspect of leadership that many lawyers don't expect is the loss of control. Lots of business owners don't want to hear this, but to grow, you have to give up control. You have to let other people do the work and accept that they won't always do it the way you would. You have to be okay with mistakes, miscommunications, and missteps. They're going to happen—call it growing pains.

Growth requires trust. It requires developing your team and then letting them develop others. If you can't learn to let go, your firm will eventually stop growing because you'll be the bottleneck. And your team, without autonomy and opportunities for growth, won't stick around.

Additionally, though, once you have staff members, they will need the autonomy to do their own work. In other words, you need to learn to delegate. This is a challenge for a lot of lawyers because many of us are perfectionists. But if you want your law firm to grow, you have to let that go. That mindset shift—learning what to let go—is a crucial part of business leadership versus the simple practice of law. We will talk more about company culture as a whole in the next chapter.

Growing Big and Strong

When your law firm is small and unproven, it appears risky to potential employees, especially the good ones, and you have less money to invest. How do you become less risky? You may have to grow.

The problem is that growing a law firm isn't easy. In my experience, getting leads is the part that worries a lot of law firm owners, but that's often the simplest part. It's what comes next—building the infrastructure to convert those leads into clients and consistently delivering on the promises you make to them—that challenges law firms. That's also where most people get stuck. You must make tough decisions, take risks, and invest time and money.

People need food, water, sleep, social interaction, and a whole slew of other elements to successfully grow. Law firms also have a lot of requirements, from a solid marketing stack to good branding and the right team of employees with the right agreements. Growing a firm requires marketing and hiring, as we covered in this chapter. You'll need to learn to hire, train, delegate, communicate, inspire, and lead your team. And that, in turn, requires mindset, leadership, and a focus on the long game.

If you want to grow, you'll need to get comfortable with risk, setbacks, self-doubt, and reinvesting in your firm even when it feels uncomfortable. Those changes take longer than you think, and they cost more than you planned.

If you're willing to embrace that, you're already halfway there. With all these elements in place, your little law firm can start to transform into something formidable. Eventually, you reach a size where you can afford to pay and appear less risky, but it's still difficult. Then you reach a critical mass and move forward in the law firm life cycle.

6. OPERATE PART I— INTERNAL WORKINGS

I wish I could say it has been smooth sailing for Law Firm GC since we began growing, but I would be lying. Many lawyers who leave an established platform to start their own firm don't realize all the work that goes into running a law firm. It turns out that included me, even though I already had some entrepreneurial aspirations.

When you're plugged into a firm as an employee, you assume that everything will work smoothly. If you need something, someone takes care of it. If you need to do something, there's a process in place and protocol to follow.

When you start a new firm, though, none of that is the case. Now you create all the processes, workflows, policies— everything that goes into business operations. This takes time, effort, and learning from your mistakes. And there will be lots of mistakes.

But after a time, the law firm begins to catch its rhythm and hum along. The growth may be slow and organic, but once you find mature equilibrium in this stage of the law firm life cycle, everything will run smoothly for you, unless some extenuating circumstance arises.

Because operations are such a huge topic, I've split this part of the life cycle into two. In this first operations chapter, we'll be covering the internal part of your operations—those having to do with your staff. From building systems and processes to creating a comprehensive employee handbook and written agreements, this chapter will go over some of the nuts and bolts of operating your law firm with an efficient and happy team.

Systems and Processes

We hear a lot about systematizing our law firms, and for good reason. Here are some of the advantages of strong systems and processes.

Less stress: Systems and processes reduce the stress of running the firm. Without systems, you have pure chaos once you start adding staff. Everyone has different ways of doing things, the paper trail is inconsistent, and everything quickly devolves into a mess that no one can fix. That's no way to run a business.

Quality and consistency: Systems enhance the quality and consistency of legal work across a firm. That way, all your attorneys do their work the way the firm decides it should be done instead of everyone completing tasks their own way.

Through systems and processes, you can teach and inform your team how to do tasks competently, stay accountable, and interact with clients consistently and at a high level.

Enhanced efficiency: Systems truly do enhance efficiency. As we enter this new age of AI and automation, efficiency will increasingly become the name of the game. The old ways—being slow and billing by the hour—will be tested. You need to be ready for that, and systems and processes will help you to move ahead with the times.

Mitigated risk: Mitigating risk is perhaps the greatest reason for investing time in creating systems and processes. If you have well-developed systems that people follow, you mitigate risks to the firm. For example, if you have systems and processes for proper calendaring of deadlines and notices that go out on a specific timeline, tasks are less likely to slip through the cracks. If you don't have well-developed systems and the technology to track everything, though, the risks to your firm go up exponentially. This is especially true as you scale.

Good online reviews: Most entrepreneurial law firms already understand how important it is to get good reviews and avoid bad ones. With systems and processes in place for both the delivery of the work and the client interaction, you can improve the client experience, get more positive reviews, and avoid bad reviews that could hurt your business.

Value of the firm: The more developed and documented your systems and processes are, the more valuable your firm becomes. They enhance your firm's value to a potential buyer because they increase efficiency, ultimately improving profitability as you operate the firm.

When the time comes to create systems and processes for your firm, you can find a lot of literature, coaches, and consultants that can help. The classic book on systems is *The E-Myth* by Michael E. Gerber. And if you want some perspective on this written specifically for attorneys, I recommend *The Power of a System* by John Fisher. Fisher himself is a practicing attorney, so his advice is perfect for those of us in this space.

The Employee Handbook

Written policies that employees, attorneys, and contractors can understand and follow are critical to a growing firm's operation. The tried-and-true location for this information is an employee handbook. It lays out the standard, legally mandated policies that apply to employees—federal and state requirements—plus anything else you need them to know.

While creating an employee handbook isn't the sexiest activity, it's important for many reasons:

- An employee handbook clearly lays out your firm's expectations for employees.
- An employee handbook makes those expectations and policies unambiguous so people know what they are required to do and what they can't do.
- An employee handbook helps when, inevitably, some issue comes up with an employee. It's much

easier to point out wrongdoing when you can indicate a clear, written policy versus saying "You should have known better."

In addition to the typical inclusions, I will highlight a couple of specific policies law firms need to address.

AI Policy

AI use is here and growing exponentially. Anyone at your firm under the age of thirty is certainly using it daily, whether you know it or not. As we all have heard by now, courts have already sanctioned multiple lawyers for filing briefs packed with hallucinated, fake cases supplied by AI.

Many firms are so scared that they have outright banned the use of AI. I don't think that's the right approach. It's certainly not one that can last. Again, people are using it, whether you tell them to or not. You're better served putting a formal policy in place to educate people about AI and let them know what is permissible and what isn't. For example, there are privacy concerns when using AI. If your staff is copying and pasting confidential client information into AI tools, they may be sharing that information with the companies that provide the AI, which can violate confidentiality rules.

Finally, remember that AI is moving so fast that this isn't a policy you can write once and file away. You need to revisit this once or even twice a year to keep up with technological advances.

Computer Use Policy

This is another policy that I have seen come into play in litigation, both in law firms and in non-law companies. Many firms don't address it adequately or at all.

Your computer use policy should address how and what your employees can and can't use firm computer systems for. It also informs your employees that they don't have an expectation of privacy when using firm computers, servers, cloud accounts, or email.

I've seen situations where a former employee is suing the firm they worked at. They had saved personal documents on the system and used their firm email to communicate with their personal lawyer outside the firm. That employee may claim privilege and say you have no right to access that information. If you don't have a written policy, you as the firm owner may lose that argument. But if you have a clear, regularly enforced computer use policy that everyone has seen and signed, you'll likely prevail on that issue and be able to access those files.

Social Media Policy

Nowadays, every law firm should have a written social media policy. Some rules are obvious, such as "Do not disclose confidential client information online," but a new twenty-year-old hire in a non-law role may not fully grasp that.

Everyone at your law firm, including non-lawyers, needs to understand that you don't go on social media and talk about clients or cases. Without guidance, a naive employee might hop on social media and share "crazy stuff" about clients. Having a social media policy that they are informed of, and they sign off on, helps reduce the chance of that occurring.

Custom and Evolving Policies

Other policies can come up over time, and you should add them as needed. My team comes up with all sorts of bespoke policies for clients, and we are constantly adding to our repertoire of policies. Sometimes we have clients come to us with a specific issue that we've never encountered before; thus, our list of custom policies keeps growing.

For example, one of our law firm clients had grown to a large team of lawyers. The owner was concerned about what would happen if an attorney, unbeknownst to him, was threatened with a sanctions motion from opposing counsel because of actions taken in litigation. The owner knew that if a court imposed sanctions, those sanctions would be against both the lawyer and the firm. The firm would then be on the hook for sanctions that it was not timely made aware of.

My team drafted a policy that contained important requirements (among other things):

- Required notice (in writing) to the firm and to the client if a motion for sanctions has been filed or is being set up to file

- Required certain disclosures to the client explaining potential adverse consequences and the potential for a conflict between the client and the firm
- Required a good faith attempt to confer with opposing counsel to resolve the underlying issue

The policy also put the responsibility for any sanctions on the attorney if they failed to provide the required notices.

Then the firm had every attorney acknowledge the policy in writing. Such a policy may not eliminate the threat of sanctions against the firm, but the likelihood of timely disclosure to the firm increases substantially when attorneys acknowledge something like this. And with early knowledge comes the potential to mitigate any adverse consequences.

When it comes to policies covered by your employee handbook, the sky's the limit. Remember to put everything in writing, make sure everyone signs and acknowledges the employee handbook policies, and enforce them consistently.

Nondisclosure Agreements and Confidentiality Agreements

Are you wondering why the previous section didn't include nondisclosure agreements (NDAs) and confidentiality agreements? Many firms I've seen include these provisions in their employee handbooks and have employees sign the handbook. That's better than nothing, but it's far better to have separate written agreements with your employees that cover this information.

You should have separate, written agreements with every member of your staff requiring them to keep client information confidential. Those same agreements should also cover firm information and trade secrets, making it unambiguous that this material may not be shared outside the firm.

Why? As attorneys, we already know that client information must remain confidential. The bar regulators are there to enforce those rules against us. The non-attorney staff may not take this as seriously as we do, even if this information is in the handbook. But when you put it in a separate agreement that is a contract, it raises the issue to the forefront for these non-lawyer employees. They see the agreement, they absorb it, and they sign it. Once it's in the agreement, and you've ensured they've read it, they can't later claim they weren't aware of the agreement. And most handbooks explicitly state they are not contracts.

There are other advantages to separating these agreements as well that we'll go over in this section. In my experience and from talking to hundreds of other lawyers, creating separate NDAs and confidentiality agreements is not yet the norm. Even so, I hope you can see why I strongly encourage my clients to use separate agreements with their non-attorney staff. When you create them, I suggest including a few specific elements for these types of agreements.

Contractual Remedies

You can embed contractual remedies in these agreements—remedies that may not be available under common law if an employee violates a policy contained in an employee handbook. Take, for example, a provision that prohibits an employee from sharing client information outside the firm. You could include a clause that prohibits employees from taking or using firm information if they leave, particularly if they go to a competitor and disclose the inner workings of your firm.

It's certainly helpful to include that in your handbook, but handbooks are generally not considered contracts and typically don't contain enforceable remedies for the firm. By contrast, if you include those same provisions in a stand-alone agreement, you can also include specific remedies for a breach. You could specify, for instance, remedies such as requiring the employee to pay certain amounts or losing their right to bonuses.

You can also include a contractual attorneys' fees provision directly in the NDA. This means that if you sue them for violating the contract and you win, they must pay your attorneys' fees. You can only do that through a contract. If you don't include these clauses in the contract, relying on basic common law remedies is much more difficult.

Written Agreements with Your Attorney Employees

If you want to grow and expand your firm, you eventually need to hire attorneys. But that comes with risks. Many—if not most—law firms don't have their attorneys sign written agreements with the firm. Some do have these agreements in place, but many that I've reviewed are often deficient or unenforceable in some way.

I think all firms need written agreements in place with attorney employees. This is extremely important regardless of what type of law you're practicing. Why? While you can't prevent attorneys from leaving with clients, if you have an agreement in place, you can minimize any potential losses.

Leaving with Clients: The Limitations of Attorney Employee Written Agreements

There are many things you can't achieve via contracts with your attorneys. A common (but not unjustified) fear of many of my law firm owner clients is that they will bring in an associate and hand them cases, only to have that attorney turn around and leave with those cases. It's true that you can't stop an attorney from leaving, and you can't prevent a client from leaving with that attorney. You also can't impose restrictive covenants, non-competes, or non-solicitation agreements on lawyers.

This presents a huge disadvantage for law firm owners who want to grow their practices. Let's say you've got a personal injury firm, and you've got an associate handling a caseload. Within that caseload, there are a couple of multimillion-dollar contingency cases. The potential fee to the firm could be in the high six figures, seven figures, maybe even eight.

You've worked hard to get those cases. It's competitive out there. These files are hard to get, and you work on them for a long time—sometimes for years—before you ever get paid. If an attorney leaves and takes the case, the firm could potentially lose millions of dollars. Multiply that by multiple attorneys over multiple years, and that number could be huge.

What an Attorney Employee Written Agreement Can Achieve

We've talked about the limitations of written contracts with your attorneys. Now, let's talk about some of the things that can be achieved. Having well-drafted, enforceable agreements with your attorneys will help minimize the risks to you and your firm.

It's not enough to have your staff attorneys sign a written agreement; it must be enforceable. I've seen agreements that said something like, "If you leave, you can't take the cases because they belong to the firm." That's not going to work. That kind of language is contrary to many ethical opinions and won't be enforced.

I've also seen provisions that say something like, "If you take cases, then all the fees that you earn from that must be paid back to the firm." Again—not enforceable. It might feel good to put that into an agreement, but that's not going to work.

That said, there are ways to draft agreements that are enforceable. If your firm handles contingency cases, you can put in place agreed-upon fee splits on cases that a departing attorney takes. These types of provisions are generally enforceable. But keep in mind that if the fee split is overly oppressive on the departing lawyer, a court may decide the provision is a financial penalty akin to an unenforceable restrictive covenant, so you need to be careful.

There are many other protective elements you should consider putting into these contracts, too, that answer some of the following questions:

- When does the attorney have to give notice to the firm that they're leaving?
- Who notifies the client?
- How will the notification be worded?
- When will the client be notified?

Other Potential Clauses

There are also provisions you can put in your attorney contracts that are unrelated to a lawyer leaving the firm with clients. These provisions are no less important. Here are a few:

- The attorney won't moonlight—meaning, they won't work for another firm or for themselves on the side.
- The attorney won't refer cases outside the firm without first running it by the firm.
- The attorney will keep firm information confidential.

There are other options as well, such as a non-disparagement clause and a dispute resolution process. You can do a lot with these agreements, and the more you do, the more you protect your business.

Compensation

You might not realize it, but many firm's compensation systems work against them. Not in the obvious ways—salaries get paid and bonuses go out—but in the subtle, more dangerous ways.

Your compensation system can shape behavior and influence what gets prioritized (and what gets ignored). Many law firms inadvertently design compensation systems that fail on many levels:

- Incentivize some, but not all, desired behaviors
- Reward short-term wins at the expense of long-term growth
- Incentivize individual performance over team success

- Overlook contributions like leadership, mentoring, or building firm culture
- Don't adequately recognize and compensate for contributions to the firm

A compensation system like that can shape the trajectory of your firm. Now, I'll admit there's no perfect law firm compensation model, but some are better than others. Start by asking the right questions:

- What behaviors should my compensation system reward?
- What behaviors should my compensation system discourage?
- How can I align incentives with the kind of firm I want to build?

Because here's the truth: Incentives drive behavior, and short-term actions have long-term consequences.

If your compensation system pushes people to focus only on today's numbers, don't be surprised when they ignore tomorrow's vision. Yes, you want performance. But you also want staying power. You want loyalty. Leadership. Collaboration. If someone performs well, you need to recognize that through your compensation system. If you don't, they probably won't stick around very long.

Therefore, as you create your compensation system, it's important to find the balance. Compensate for what matters—not merely what's easy to measure. Because if you get this right, the future of your firm will follow. If you don't, you may be quietly undermining everything you're trying to build.

Trust Accounting

Most lawyers understand what a trust account is. This special bank account holds funds that belong to clients or third parties. Depending on the jurisdiction, trust accounts are often called an IOLTA (Interest on Lawyers' Trust Account) or IOTA (Interest on Trust Account).

If you're holding client money or third-party funds in your law firm, then you are required to use a trust account. Let's say I bring on a new client and ask for a retainer. Since I haven't earned that retainer yet, it must go into the trust account. Then, when I send a bill and earn some of that fee, I can transfer the money into the firm's operating account.

Here's another scenario: I receive a personal injury settlement. I then deposit it into my firm's trust account and disburse the funds owed to the client, medical providers, and my firm from the trust account.

Trust accounting may be boring, but you need to take it seriously because the ramifications of not doing so are enormous. Until you've earned the money and transferred it to the firm, it's still the client's money. This means it needs to be handled with extra care:

- You cannot co-mingle client funds with firm funds
- You cannot deposit your own money into the trust account

The trust account should contain only client or third-party funds.

I've seen unfortunate situations, like an attorney who has a cash flow issue and thinks, *I have this money in the trust account. I'll borrow it for now, and I'll pay it back later.* Huge mistake—one that can get you suspended or disbarred. Handle your trust account with care, and don't give unfettered access to any of your employees. If they steal money from that account, you are on the hook for it.

Mental Health

The practice of law is extremely stressful. In this career, you're working hard and constantly taking on other people's problems. If you're not careful, that stress can break you down. And if you break down, and you're the owner of your firm, your firm might go down with you.

A study by the American Bar Association and Hazelden Betty Ford Foundation found that nearly 21 percent of lawyers qualify as problem drinkers, with that number rising to over 36 percent when more detailed questions were asked. The same study found that more than 45 percent of attorneys experience depression during their careers and nearly 12 percent reporting suicidal thoughts at some point. To cap it all off, 9 percent of attorneys report struggling with prescription drug abuse, often using substances to manage stress, stay awake, or sleep.[4]

There can be a tendency among lawyers to lean toward alcohol or substances to cope with some of that stress. In fact, alcohol and drug abuse rates among lawyers are significantly higher than in many other professions. Suicide rates are high too. Tragically high.[5] Why? Because the pressure never lets up. When that pressure builds, some lawyers lean on alcohol or substances as a coping mechanism.

I know of a firm where an attorney had a hidden alcohol problem. She was struggling quietly, and no one at the firm knew until it was too late. She ended up committing malpractice on multiple cases. The fallout was massive.

I hope you can see that it's crucial that lawyers take care of themselves in healthy ways. If you or your attorneys aren't healthy, then your firm is at risk. Whether it's exercise, meditation, sleep, hobbies, or vacations, you've got to find

4   Priscilla Henson, MD, "Addiction & Substance Abuse in Lawyers: Statistics to Know," American Addiction Centers, updated January 28, 2025, https://americanaddictioncenters.org/workforce-addiction/white-collar/lawyers.

5   Don G. Rushing and Andrew B. Serwin, "Pathways to Wellness in the Practice of Law," *The Bencher*—March/April 2020, American Inns of Court, accessed June 19, 2025, https://home.innsofcourt.org/AIC/AIC_For_Members/AIC_Bencher/AIC_Bencher_Recent_Articles/2020_MarApr_Rushing-Serwin.aspx.

your outlet. For me, that's the gym; I make sure to go every morning to blow off steam before work.

Build healthy routines. Prioritize time off. And don't just focus on yourself—make sure your attorneys and staff are okay too. This goes back to the importance of a good company culture. You've got to create an environment where people can speak up without fear. If someone is dealing with a problem, they need to feel safe coming forward. You can't punish people for asking for help; you need to encourage them to take care of themselves. A healthy owner and a healthy team are much more likely to run a healthy law firm.

An Inside Operation

Operating a firm can be overwhelming. You have to do all the work normal businesses do, like create strong systems and processes, a good company culture, and a comprehensive employee handbook. But you also need to take extra precautions to protect sensitive information, create policies for any attorneys on your staff, and model healthy stress management for your team (and encourage them to take care of themselves as well). Only with all that internal structure in place can you serve the people outside your firm—your customers. That's what we will tackle in the next chapter.

7. OPERATE PART II— EXTERNAL THREATS

When you're operating a law firm, you have to deal with a variety of external threats. They come from all sorts of places. They come from your clients. They come from vendors, landlords, creditors, co-counsel, cybercriminals, bar regulators, third parties. Although we don't have space to discuss them all, this chapter is about dealing with external threats.

Clients are the lifeblood of your firm, and you work hard to bring them in. But they also constitute a threat if you don't take the right precautions. In this chapter, our primary focus is on clients—signing them on, talking to them, and dealing with complaints. Once you've got their attention, you have to think about everything from how to design an ironclad client retainer agreement to how to communicate with clients and what to do if things go awry. You must cultivate a growth mindset, remain adaptable, and prepare to wear multiple hats, particularly in the early stages. We will also leave some space to talk about other threats, including a relatively new one: cybercriminals.

Client Retainer Agreement / Engagement Letter

Once you've determined that you can move ahead with a client, it's time to draft a client retainer agreement. Client retainer agreements are a law firm's first line of defense with respect to their clients. A strong client retainer agreement sets the tone for the professional relationship. More than just a formal requirement, it helps establish expectations— what the client can expect from the firm and what the firm expects from the client.

These expectations should always be put in writing. If the relationship deteriorates or a dispute like a bar complaint arises, a signed agreement can serve as critical protection for your firm.

There are key elements that every client retainer agreement should include. But before we get into those, I want to remind you that a client retainer agreement isn't a set-it-and-forget-it deal. You must customize your agreement for each client, and most lawyers know to get a signed engagement agreement when a new client first comes in. But they often forget that every *new* matter—every *new* engagement—needs a new agreement. This applies even if the engagement is with someone you've already worked with and have an agreement on file for.

Clients come back, the work evolves, and the original agreement doesn't always cover what you're now doing. Best practice: Get a new retainer agreement every time. That may sound tedious, but it protects everyone involved and allows you to tailor the agreement to the specific matter at hand.

Who the Client Is

Knowing who the client is seems obvious, but it's easy to get wrong, and clarity on client identity helps you avoid ethical pitfalls and conflicts later. Here are two common scenarios.

Business or individual: Let's say a business owner approaches you. Who are you representing: the business or the individual owners? And which owners are you representing if there are multiple owners?

Parent or teen/adult child: If you're representing a minor, you'll need a parent or guardian to sign on their behalf. But once that minor becomes an adult, you need a new agreement with the now-adult client.

Scope of the Engagement

Ambiguity around scope can lead to serious problems, so be specific about what you are (and are not) being hired to do. Tax advice is an excellent example of this. Suppose you're hired to handle a business deal but not to give tax advice. You run a small firm and don't have a tax expert on staff. This is not uncommon; most of the time, only large firms have specialized tax professionals. Many smaller law firms don't need them as long as they're being transparent about what they offer. For instance, a small commercial real estate lawyer without an on-staff tax specialist might handle a $20 million deal for a client.

This arrangement can backfire if you don't clearly define the scope of your engagement. There have been major malpractice cases tied to massive deals—I'm talking hundreds of millions or even a billion dollars—that weren't structured in a way that minimized taxes. Those can end up costing a client tens or even hundreds of millions in unnecessary tax liability.

You will likely not be conducting billion-dollar deals, but the concept is the same. If you don't clearly state in your engagement letter that you do not give tax advice, that client may come back later and blame you for negative tax consequences. But if your engagement letter says, "We are not providing tax advice; please consult with a tax advisor," you've protected yourself.

Potential Conflicts

If you've gotten to the point of signing an agreement, you've already ruled out any conflicts that would keep the client from working with you. But if there are any known or potential conflicts that require a waiver, you must get them in writing and have the client sign. For instance, if you're representing two clients (like business partners or co-defendants) in related matters, you'll need a written waiver confirming they understand and accept the potential for divided loyalty. The engagement letter is the right place to handle this, as you don't want to be in a position later where the client claims they weren't fully informed.

Conflict of Interest with Clients

When it comes to clients, the first question is simple: Who are they? You need to think about who you can and can't represent in the first place.

Lawyers must be on guard about potential client conflicts. You likely don't need me to remind you that you can't represent clients on both sides of a lawsuit. I can't represent both Susie and Johnny, because my fiduciary duties—my loyalty—would be split between the two of them. Everybody knows that, and while that situation seems simple enough, conflicts of interest can get complicated fast.

Maybe you have a lawyer who represents a client in one matter, and you've got another lawyer down the hall who represents a different client who is suing the first client. While this situation seems more convoluted and is harder to spot, it is also considered improper.

There are five hundred–page books written on conflicts of interest, and I don't want to be here for five hundred pages, so we're not going to go too deep here. Be aware that it's important to stay on top of conflicts analysis from a risk management standpoint. When you see a conflict, you must turn that potential client away. I know it's tough to turn away clients, especially when you have multiple attorneys in your firm. You'll be tempted to figure out a way to make it work, but I strongly advise against this. You could end up losing both clients or getting sued by both clients, and the risk isn't worth it.

Your Expectations for the Client

Just as a client has expectations for their lawyer, you have expectations for the client. For instance, they must agree to cooperate with you, remaining communicative and showing up for appointments and court dates during the representation.

If you've practiced long enough, you've likely encountered the client who disappears. They ghost you—no calls returned, no replies to emails—and yet the matter is still moving forward. That puts you, the attorney, in a difficult spot. So address it up front, by spelling it out in the engagement letter and indicating what will happen if they fail to uphold their end of the deal.

The client also needs to let you know if they change their address, their circumstances change, or they file for bankruptcy.

No Guarantees

I always include another detail—what I call "the magic words": There are no guarantees of success. Some version of that language should appear in every engagement letter. There is no guarantee you'll win. And no matter what you say, some clients will convince themselves that you promised a particular outcome. If it's in writing—and they signed it—you can point to that clause and say, "No, I did not guarantee anything."

Fees and Costs (Contingency and Non-Contingency)

You also need to clearly explain fees and costs. How are fees calculated? Who pays for which costs and expenses? This is particularly critical in contingency matters since you don't get paid up-front. It's more than best practice; you need to put it in your client retainer agreement.

In contingency cases, attorneys often advance expenses. If there's a recovery, the client is responsible for those expenses. You need to explain this to the client. Does repayment happen before or after the contingency fee is calculated? Be clear and write it out, because even though we as lawyers think it's obvious, clients don't have our background. Naturally, they won't understand any of this unless you tell them.

For non-contingency matters, clarify whether a retainer is required. Is it a replenishing retainer? Are there interest charges on late payments? How will you bill the client? All this goes into the fees section of your client agreement.

Arbitration Provision

Arbitration provisions in attorney-client agreements are not permitted in every US state. Your first step here, therefore, is to check your jurisdiction and confirm whether arbitration clauses are even allowed in your state.

If arbitration provisions are allowed, think carefully about how to word the provision. I've seen arbitration clauses that are only a line or two—something like "Any dispute will be arbitrated." That kind of language will not hold up in most jurisdictions.

In states where arbitration is permitted, most apply some form of an *informed consent* standard. That means you must clearly explain what the client is agreeing to. What rights are they giving up? How does arbitration work? Who pays for what? What's the structure of the process? All of that needs to be spelled out in detail to satisfy the informed consent requirement.

Another important point: In most states that allow arbitration provisions in attorney-client agreements, the clause must be *initialed* by both the attorney and the client. So even if your language is perfect, if it's not initialed, you may still be out of luck.

The takeaway: If you're going to include an arbitration clause, you must check whether it's allowed in your state, you must draft it in a way that's enforceable, and you must make sure you meet all the requirements for enforceability—including initials if required.

Client Communication: Enhancing the Client Experience

Nobody wants to hire a lawyer. In most cases, something bad has happened in their life, and hiring a lawyer is the unfortunate result. To many people, lawyers and the law are intimidating. You live in the legal world every day, but your clients don't, and unknowns can be frightening. What's second nature to you is a mystery to them.

The mystery is compounded by the way retaining an attorney works. For a client, the law isn't like buying an iPhone; they don't unwrap a product and start using it. A client hires a lawyer, and then the case disappears into a black box. Occasionally, something pops out, but the whole process is convoluted. The client doesn't know what's happening, if you're working or not, unless you tell them.

Regular communication makes an enormous difference here. It keeps the client in the loop, letting them know what has happened, what's happening now, and what's going to happen. And when doing so, remember that you must be sensitive to the client experience and understand what they're going through. Clients are stressed out. They're in unfamiliar territory, and they're going through something hard. So talk to them regularly, and talk to them with empathy.

I have one specific tip for you here: A key part of good client communication is avoiding legal jargon. If you tell a client, "We're going to file a motion for summary judgment," they won't understand because they didn't go to law school. Remember to talk to them in layman's terms. Keep it clear; keep it simple.

Communication Lessens Chances of Complaints

This regular, kind client communication isn't all about benevolence. That experience affects your reputation, your reviews—your entire brand. A study in the *Western Journal of Medicine* about medical malpractice claims showed that the number one predictor of whether a doctor would get sued wasn't the outcome or even whether something went wrong. Instead, it was how long the doctor spent talking with the patient. The more time the doctor spent with the patient, the lower the likelihood of a lawsuit became. People felt like they had a relationship, and that made a difference.[6]

The same dynamic likely applies in law. Most sources suggest that a top reason clients file bar complaints is due to poor or nonexistent communication.[7] Thus, from the standpoint of avoiding bar complaints alone, it's critical to communicate with your client early and often.

Podcast Feature: James Joseph on Billing and Getting Paid

James Joseph runs a matrimonial firm on Long Island, which he started five years out of law school in 1998. But

---

6   Philip J. Moore, Nancy E. Adler, and Patricia A. Robertson, "Medical Malpractice: The Effect of Doctor-Patient Relations on Medical Patient Perceptions and Malpractice Intentions," *Western Journal of Medicine* 173, no. 4 (October 2000): 244, accessed June 18, 2025, https://www.ncbi.nlm.nih.gov/pmc/articles/PMC1071103/.

7   Susan Buckner and Melissa Bender, "Lawyer Complaints" FindLaw, 2023, https://www.findlaw.com/hirealawyer/choosing-the-right-lawyer/lawyer-complaints.html.

he got his start at a firm as an associate. That firm seemed successful—they got lots of clients and did lots of good work—but the partners were terrible businesspeople who never collected money.

On *Founding Partner Podcast*, James relayed a story about getting paid. "[My boss] said to me, 'How much do you think I should be paying you?' And I said, 'Honestly, double.' And he said to me, 'You're right, but we have no money. We can't pay our bills.'"

And that's when it dawned on James that a law firm is, ultimately, a business. He learned several valuable lessons from this.

Avoid Taking Every Client

"The partner that was in charge of that side of the practice was a really decent, nice guy who cared deeply about people," James explained to me. "And we represented, as often happens when you start a matrimonial practice, friends and family and his friends. The bulk of them, at the time, didn't have a lot of money. . . . Divorce is expensive, and he felt bad charging them."

Unfortunately, this seemingly benevolent approach backfired. Many lawyers, like James's former bosses, argue that law is a profession—a calling to help clients. That's all well and good, but if you don't get paid, you're not going to be able to help anybody. "We had to take on a lot of extra business because there was no money," James explained. "We would accept any case that came in regardless of whether they could afford to pay us in full, regardless of whether they were reasonable, whether their goals were reasonable, and we could never get the work done."

James learned that doing well financially gives a legal practice the opportunity to help more people. This, in turn, means that you need to charge what you're worth and get paid for the work you do as much as possible.

Track Time and Collections Diligently

At his former workplace, James saw firsthand how poor billing, no client screening, and disorganized operations can jeopardize financial stability. He said that when he first started at that former firm, "I said to [my boss], 'I've never billed before. How does it work?' And he said, 'Well, we're generally here twelve hours a day; try to capture four.' And that boss was probably billing half of those hours."

This was no way to run a firm. "They didn't know anything about the importance of client selection, of billing, of collecting," he said of his former bosses. "That was one of the really valuable lessons."

When Things Go Wrong

Clear and consistent communication with the client is a risk mitigation strategy, but it doesn't eliminate risks. Sometimes, despite your best efforts, things go wrong. Clients will fire you, leave negative reviews, or even accuse you of malpractice. This section is about what to do if you ever find yourself in these situations.

If You Get Fired: The Client File, Retaining Liens, and Contingency Cases

For the most part, clients have a right to discharge their attorney at any time and for any reason. If that happens, clients retain certain rights. We as attorneys are bound by a number of ethical and procedural obligations regardless of the reason for the discharge.

If a client fires you and asks for their file, you are almost always required to provide it. You can't refuse to hand it over. That said, most jurisdictions have what's called a retaining lien, which allows a lawyer to hold a client's file until unpaid legal fees are settled. In other words, if the client owes you money, you can, in theory, withhold the file until you are paid. But be careful!

Even in jurisdictions that recognize retaining liens, ethical rules often limit their practical use. For example, you can't withhold a client's file if doing so would prejudice the client. If, say, the client is in active litigation with a hearing in three weeks and needs the file for new counsel, you can't ethically refuse to hand it over because of nonpayment. Doing so would certainly prejudice the case.

In contingency cases, the file issue becomes even murkier. Suppose you're representing someone injured in a car wreck, and your fee is contingent on the outcome. If the client fires you mid-case and hires a new attorney, the fired lawyer may feel little incentive to promptly release the file.

For the client's new attorney, this leads to significant delays. If your firm drags its feet, taking weeks to release the file, you might end up with several follow-ups, threats, or letters. Some firms may even use this as leverage against the attorney who left. While this behavior may be common, it isn't appropriate. Intentionally withholding a file to delay or disadvantage the client or successor counsel—whether for leverage, out of spite, or as a pressure tactic—can expose you and your firm to serious professional risk. Slow-walking is common, perhaps because the firm is busy, perhaps for other reasons.

Even if a lien exists and payment is due, ethical obligations usually come first. The better (and safer) practice is to promptly turn over the file, preserve the client's interests, and address the financial issues separately. This helps to preserve your reputation and ethical track record, even if you were discharged for reasons you feel were unfair.

Negative Reviews: Should You Respond?

Today, potential clients often find law firms online. Reviews play a leading role in shaping your reputation. Platforms like Google, Avvo, Yelp, and Facebook matter; clients read them. A single negative review can damage your reputation and hurt business development.

This happens all the time. I know of one incident where a client who refused to take their lawyer's advice—and then refused to pay—was fired by the firm. That client later posted a negative review and mobilized a Facebook group to flood the firm's page with fake one-star reviews from people who had never interacted with the firm. It severely impacted that firm's reputation and took a lot of damage control to fix.

That brings me to another important issue—not all negative reviews come from clients. Sometimes they come from coordinated campaigns, like the one I described, where one disgruntled person encourages others—who have never been clients—to post false one-star reviews. Sometimes they come from non-clients who had a brief or unsatisfactory interaction with your staff, from opposing parties in litigation, from former employees, or from your competitors.

How to Respond to Negative Reviews

If someone unjustly lambasts you in a review, the natural reaction is to respond and set the record straight. But lawyers must tread carefully. There are ethical limitations on what you can say when responding to negative reviews, even when they are false or malicious.

First, when it comes to responding to reviews, you must respect client confidentiality. Even if a client disparages you publicly, you can't respond by disclosing confidential or privileged information to defend yourself. While you are permitted to respond, the ethical boundaries are strict, and any violation could lead to disciplinary action. Your reply must be restrained and carefully worded to avoid prejudicing the client in any way. This is true even if the review is false, unfair, or misleading.

Instead, a safe and ethical approach might include a general response indicating that you disagree with the review, or an invitation to the reviewer to contact the office privately to resolve any concerns. In either case, avoid any detail that might confirm the individual was a client.

Many states have issued ethics opinions on this subject. North Carolina has issued 2020 Formal Ethics Opinion 1, which provides a comprehensive discussion on a lawyer's ability to respond to negative online reviews. The opinion even includes a discussion on situations involving people who consulted with the lawyer but never became clients.[8] The inquiry states that in such cases, since no attorney-client relationship exists, there is no duty of confidentiality. That means a lawyer can respond more freely, though still with professionalism and caution.

North Carolina extends this principle to reviews left by friends or relatives of a client. Because these individuals were never clients themselves, lawyers may again be more candid—though still within the bounds of professionalism and ethical obligations.

That said, even when ethics rules allow a broader response, exercise caution not to "throw the client under the bus." A defensive or emotional reply can often do more harm than good, and taking the high road often pays off.

---

8   "2020 Formal Ethics Opinion 1: Responding to Negative On-
    line Reviews," North Carolina State Bar, adopted July 16, 2021,
    accessed June 18, 2025, https://www.ncbar.gov/for-lawyers/
    ethics/adopted-opinions/2020-formal-ethics-opinion-1/.

Should I Report a False Review?

In an ideal world, if a review contains false or defamatory claims, you could get the platform to remove it. Unfortunately, anyone who has gone through this process knows that getting Google (or most other review platforms) to take down a review is extraordinarily difficult, even when you provide evidence that the reviewer was never a client or that the review is patently false. While there are rare cases where removal occurs, you can't rely on it as a viable solution.

As a result, many consultants and marketing professionals recommend a different approach. Rather than focusing your efforts on removing a negative review, address it with a bland, professional response that doesn't reveal any confidential information, and then work to dilute its impact. An effective way to do this is by generating a stream of positive reviews from satisfied clients. A strong collection of positive feedback can outweigh and mitigate the damage of a single negative post, so be sure to ask your satisfied clients to leave reviews.

Suing Clients

Sometimes clients act in such a way that the only answer is litigation. There are all sorts of reasons why a firm may be tempted to sue a client, but some major ones come up regularly: unpaid fees (the client didn't pay, and the firm wants to get paid) and negative reviews (the firm contends that a harsh online review is false and defamatory).

I have helped firms sue clients for both these reasons. Clients owed large sums—six figures—and the firm sued and got paid. I have also seen suits over defamatory reviews succeed and force those reviews down. Even so, I don't typically recommend suing: (1) If you sue, you will likely be countersued for an alleged breach of fiduciary duty or malpractice. This is a high risk that you must be prepared to deal with. (2) When you sue a client, your malpractice insurance renewal becomes more complicated. Renewal applications often ask, "Have you ever sued your client?" Insurers know that firms willing to sue clients face a higher likelihood of malpractice claims, and your underwriting can change (usually not in your favor).

Most of the time, suing a client isn't worth it. I have also seen lawsuits backfire, and even if they don't, the downsides are significant. It may be better to hold your nose, walk away, and stay angry than to sue a client. The time, money, stress, and heartache of litigation are generally much higher than the potential rewards.

I have experienced this myself. Years ago, a business client owed me well over six figures. He was wealthy, assured me he would pay, and then failed to do so. It still makes me angry to think about, but I decided it wasn't worth suing, and I walked away. I have no doubt that I made the right decision, *and* I learned a valuable lesson about billing policies in the process.

Prevention is the best medicine. Ideally, you avoid a situation where you're tempted to sue a client. If they stop paying you, you need to get out of the case. Don't let it go on, no matter how much they promise you. It is far better to cut bait and get out than it is to keep going and let those bills accumulate.

Malpractice Insurance Policies

In most states, malpractice insurance isn't required for law firms. I know of lawyers who purposely don't get it because they believe it puts a target on their back to get sued. Although it isn't required and might be seen as a bad-luck charm, I still think every law firm should buy malpractice insurance. It's not that expensive, and it gives you protection from a malpractice claim.

As an added benefit, most malpractice policies provide coverage for bar complaints. If you practice long enough, you're probably going to get a bar complaint. Most of the time, those complaints have no basis and are without merit. But an insurance policy that will pay an attorney to handle it for you is an enormous help if that situation arises. Therefore, I advise you to skip the superstition and buy the insurance.

Navigating Your Annual Renewal Application

Malpractice insurance is generally renewed annually, and that comes with a renewal application. When you're in a small firm with one or two attorneys, it's not a big deal. But as your firm grows, the chances of your renewal application going awry increase.

Let's say you've got forty attorneys at your firm. Often, one of the questions on the renewal application is "Are you aware of any claim that's been made against the firm, potential claim that's been made against the firm, or any bar grievance that's been filed against the firm?" The person filling out the application might think the answer is no, and say no—but another attorney at the firm may be aware of something they aren't.

I've seen scenarios where the owner didn't know about an incident involving an attorney on their staff. But because of how "insured" is defined in some policies, that attorney's knowledge was imputed to the firm. And so the firm lost coverage.

If you have more than a handful of attorneys working for you, I recommend you have every attorney on your staff fill out an internal survey prior to the submission of the renewal application. You can ask everyone some key questions using that survey that can save you and the firm a major headache later.

For my clients, we've gone a step further and made it a sworn statement. All attorneys must sign under oath that they aren't aware of any action against the firm. This might seem extreme, but before we started doing a sworn statement, a client had an incident where an attorney wasn't forthcoming and didn't disclose something they knew about. They essentially lied on the form, and as a result, my client ran into trouble with their insurer.

Having the survey signed under oath elevates the importance of accuracy, but there's another silver lining as well. It could give the owner of the firm some protection if the insurance company tries to deny coverage. You can at least say, "My firm did everything it could. We got signed statements, and we still didn't know." That precaution could help preserve your coverage in that situation.

There are certain policy riders you can request to prevent that exact scenario. Most people aren't aware of them; I wasn't aware of them until I ran into a situation where those exclusions were necessary for a client. For example, you can include a rider that severs imputed knowledge from the firm. This would protect you in case of a situation involving an attorney committing malpractice who hid their deeds like the one we discussed.

Even some insurance brokers aren't aware of these. But now you know they exist, and you have to ask for them. This is a perfect example of the "unknown unknowns," and it's one of the advantages of working with someone like me.

Protecting Against Other External Threats

Clients aren't the only threats to a law firm. Many other third parties pose risks as well. From other lawyers—whether they be co-counsel, predecessor counsel, or successor counsel—to landlords, vendors, and thieves, there is a lot to protect yourself from. Here are two areas to consider: co-counsel / referring counsel and cybercriminals.

Co-counsel / Referring Counsel

I'll briefly address co-counsel situations. The co-counsel agreement is a separate agreement from the written attorney employee agreement; it's connected specifically to a co-counsel case and is particularly relevant for contingency firms.

It's common for firms to co-counsel or refer cases to each other. Typically, the arrangement is informal, often involving a handshake or an email that explains how the fee will be split. Such an arrangement isn't enough, though, because lawyers try to retroactively change those deals all the time, especially in contingency work. Say I refer a $10 million case to you. You tell me, "All right, I'll give you thirty percent of whatever I recover," and we shake hands or maybe exchange an email. That's it. No formal agreement.

Fast forward eighteen months. You get a $5 million check. "Hey, Hawkins," you say. "Thanks for that referral. Here's one hundred thousand dollars." You don't pay what you originally promised. Then the situation turns into a huge fight.

People go back on their word. They get greedy, and they refuse to pay what was agreed upon. They may also engage in other forms of professional shenanigans. And when no written agreement is in place, you can't do much about it. The person who referred the case is usually the one who ends up getting burned.

The best way to protect yourself in these situations is to use written co-counsel agreements. These protect you from potentially getting swindled by the other attorney, and it can potentially help you if you ever have to go to court. Having a written agreement is much better than a handshake, an email, or a phone call. It doesn't have to be overly complicated, but it should be in writing.

Cyberattacks

Cyberattacks are another external, third-party risk. Every day, these attacks are becoming a bigger deal. That's why it's crucial that you train your staff to ward off cyber threats—and get insurance in case something slips through the cracks.

Law firms are known as "soft targets" among hackers and cybercriminals. Hackers know we hold a lot of valuable, private client information, and so law firms are often targeted and breached.

The weakest points in your system—the "soft points"—are your employees. And yes, that includes the lawyers. The sophistication of phishing emails today is insane, and anyone can fall prey to one of these scams. Emails that look like they're from one of your employees asking you to change direct deposit information can be from a hacker. Or a scammer will send an attachment that, when clicked, lets them into the system.

Train yourself and your employees. If someone's defenses go down, and they click on that weird email attachment, your whole computer system may be at risk.

This isn't what I do personally, but I do think it's worth mentioning: Most third-party information technology companies provide cybersecurity training as part of their services. And not just training—they'll also *test* your team. They send test emails for your employees and give them scores. If the employees fail, they are assigned additional training. This can be helpful if you need an extra layer of protection.

If You Experience a Breach

If something does happen and your system is compromised, you need professional assistance. A data security attorney can give you advice on your obligations about responding. Every state has its own rules about when you're required to notify your clients that there has been a breach, so this is not a good DIY project. Cyber insurance can help pay your legal fees, tech team, and anything else you need to do to remedy the situation.

Protect Your Firm

Most law firm owners focus the majority of their attention, energy, and money on increasing revenue. They might be generating leads, bringing in more cases, or going after bigger cases. Few of these law firm owners, however, give much thought to preventing their hard-earned revenue from quietly vanishing.

That's exactly where a solid risk management program factors into firm operations. Risk management helps you prepare for external threats so more of your income stays in your pocket. Whether you're checking for conflicts of interest, designing a comprehensive client retainer agreement, or responding tactfully to a disparaging review, external operations are all about the people you work for.

With the right safeguards in place, including good communication policies and malpractice insurance, you can keep these external operations running as smoothly as possible. It may not be the flashiest part of running a practice, but operations that factor in external threats are just as important as bringing in new business. After all, there's no point in bringing in new business if your earnings keep sliding through your fingers.

8. MERGERS AND ACQUISITIONS

The human life cycle often includes marriage. For law firms, the concept is less romantic. Law firm mergers and acquisitions, like marriage, can be complicated—they involve people and paperwork.

I have seen mergers—including combinations of firms, practice groups, and individual lawyers—from all sides of the equation. Before I started my own firm, I moved between firms maybe three or four times.

That fresh start can be exciting. Once, I was coming out of a firm that was dissolving, and starting somewhere new was energizing. I didn't know anyone at the new firm, so there was that element of surprise as well. You have to get to know people and prove yourself again, which is a motivator. Associates and even partners can get stuck in a routine, and sometimes change just feels good.

From the perspective of the business owner—the lawyer who is expanding the firm—it's even more galvanizing. You're growing, working toward your goals and vision. You bring in new blood, new expertise, new capabilities—and presumably, new revenue. The pie gets bigger, and so do you.

Mergers can come in different sizes. At times, it's entire firms coming together, or it can be smaller groups—subsets—merging into existing firms. The larger they are, the more difficult and logistically challenging they become. This chapter will explore (1) why firms merge or make acquisitions at any level, (2) acquisitions and mergers, and (3) firm integration issues, and the risks involved when two firms decide to tie the knot.

Why Firms Merge

Law firm mergers happen for many reasons, both good and bad. And though the reasons vary, you can usually distill them down to two categories: strategy and necessity.

Strategy

Strategic mergers are all about growth and positioning, which are really two sides of the same coin. Let's say I'm a firm that's based out of state, and I want to establish an in-state presence. I could send over an attorney and build out a new office from the ground up, but that's a lot of work. Alternatively, I could find an existing firm that would merge into my firm and become our local office. That's a strategic move that helps me accomplish a goal, and the same logic can be used to add practice area capabilities.

On the flip side, there are smaller firms that want to punch in a higher weight class. Maybe they're doing good work but feel limited in their reach or resources. They therefore start looking for a larger firm—or a firm in another market—to merge with.

Other times, competitors decide they're better off together. They look around and realize, "If we come together, we'll both be stronger than we are on our own." That's the 1 + 1 = 3 idea, and it can really pay off.

Finally, a law firm owner might get tired of running the operations/administrative side of a law firm and want to only practice law. Perhaps they're getting older, or maybe they didn't consider how much busywork being a business owner would entail. Either way, merging their firm with another firm that can handle daily operations can free up that lawyer to focus on the law again without dissolving their firm.

Necessity

Then there's the other side of it—necessity. Some firms don't have a succession plan, and when the founders start looking to retire or exit, the only way to do that and keep the firm going is to merge into another firm. That's a common approach. Oftentimes, when law firm owners neglect the transition planning, merging is their only path forward.

I've also seen firms that are bleeding out. It's a sad but common story: A big firm has a solid several decades, and then people start leaving in droves. Suddenly, it feels like a hole has been ripped into the side of the Titanic. To save themselves from the sinking ship, the partners need to find a firm to merge with to stabilize their business.

The Eleven-Step Merger Process

A merger is much more complicated than signing a contract. So much happens before the deal, and there's a whole process *after* it if you want the merger to succeed. It takes time, effort, and careful planning. Generally, the process involves eleven steps and a lot of elbow grease.

Step 1: Identifying a Target. At a high level, the process usually starts when someone identifies a target. That could be a firm looking to acquire or to be acquired. Sometimes this happens through headhunters or brokers who are shopping firms around. There are even listings where firms are for sale.

Step 2: Making an Approach. Once a target is identified (or maybe both sides find each other), the parties begin with initial conversations. This step is like a first date, where everyone is figuring out whether there's going to be a second. All the inquiries are surface level, such as "Are you interested? What would this look like? What's your culture like? Do we like each other?"

Step 3: Early Disclosures and Nondisclosure Agreement (NDA). If the initial conversations go well, the proceedings get more serious. You are now "dating." At this point, both sides usually sign a mutual NDA. That allows everyone to be more open and share deeper information. You begin doing some light due diligence and disclosures—not everything, but more than the first round.

Step 4: Letter of Intent (LOI). If there's still interest after the initial due diligence, one party usually sends out an LOI. This is your "engagement." The LOI outlines the general terms of the potential deal and signals a commitment to continue discussions seriously.

Step 5: Deeper Due Diligence. Following the LOI, the parties dive into deeper due diligence. This is where you flesh out everything, including financials, operations, liabilities, staffing, clients, systems. You're looking under the hood to see exactly what you're merging with.

Step 6: Negotiating the Deal. If everything still looks good, the parties move on to drafting and negotiating the deal documents. These are the formal agreements that lay out the final terms of the merger.

Step 7: Signing the Deal. Once the terms are agreed to and the documents are finalized, you sign the deal. That's the formal close of the transaction—you're officially "married." But you're not done yet.

Step 8: Internal Communication. After the deal is signed, you roll it out to the rest of the firm. Most of the staff and attorneys probably weren't involved in the negotiations, so there's a whole process of informing them, answering questions, and managing reactions.

Step 9: Client Notification. Next, you notify clients. That usually involves formal letters that explain the merger and give clients the option to continue with the new firm or move elsewhere. This step is required in many cases.

Step 10: Logistics and Operations. Once clients are notified, all the logistics come into play. That includes technology integration, file transfers, administrative setup, financial data imports, billing system alignment, and onboarding employees into the new firm's infrastructure. All your systems must be merged, and often the two firms operate on different platforms. You therefore must pick a system. Everyone has to get on board with that decision, and that usually involves training, coordination, and a fair amount of logistical effort. It's a lot of work, and it takes time.

Step 11: Cultural Integration. Last but definitely not least is culture. Do not take this lightly; cultural integration is often harder than the deal itself. You've moved in together, you're sharing space, and you must make sure the two firms synergize. A merger's success ultimately comes down to the people. It's not about the numbers. It's not about the clients. It's not about the technology. It's about whether the people can work together. This includes values, communication styles, workflows, and expectations.

Acquisitions

At some point in a firm's evolution, it may want to acquire laterals, practice groups, or entire firms. On the other hand, you may lead a firm or group that is being acquired. I joined my last firm through an acquisition, where a small group of us joined the firm.

An acquisition isn't as complex as a larger-scale merger, but adding a new subset or practice group still means carefully vetting each lawyer involved in that small firm. Here are some things that both the acquirer and the acquired should consider.

Acquirers

First, you'll want to ask each of your new potential hires for two pieces of information: a resume/bio and economic data.

The resume/bio should include a comprehensive description of legal and non-legal employment in reverse chronology as well as educational background, including degrees, academic awards, and publications. The resume should also include, or attach separately, a list of representative matters.

The economic data should encompass a three-year annual history of originations and collections and a revenue projection for the first year of employment, including a minimum, reasonably expected, and optimistic prediction.

The rest of the information you'll need is more nuanced. Whether through interviews, references, or some other means, try to glean the following information about the group as a whole.

Practice fit and client transition: When evaluating a candidate during a law firm acquisition, the first step is understanding how their practice aligns with the acquiring firm's existing services. Can the firm support the candidate's clients in other areas? Are those clients likely to follow the candidate, or are they loyal to their current counsel? You should also note whether the candidate can serve any of the firm's existing clients and whether their presence could create any conflicts of interest.

Long-term outlook and adaptability: Consider the sustainability of the candidate's practice. What is the financial outlook for the industries they serve? Are there any upcoming legislative, regulatory, or judicial developments that could impact their work? And if needed, can the group pivot by learning new practice areas or adjusting to changes in the legal landscape? This flexibility is often critical to a firm's long-term success.

Risk and professional history: You'll need to thoroughly review the candidate's professional background. Ask whether anyone in the group has faced disciplinary action, been involved in litigation or administrative proceedings, or been sanctioned by a court. Don't forget about malpractice claims, client disputes, or billing issues. Finally, find out if anyone in the group has ever been asked to leave a firm or been involved in any employment-related disputes. Any red flags should be addressed early to avoid surprises later.

Integration expectations: Do you know what the new group will need for integration? What kind of office space, technology, and support staff do they expect? Are they bringing a team with them, and does the firm have the capacity to support that team? Clarify what roles or titles they're pursuing—whether they expect to lead a practice group, take on a management role, or focus on client work. And don't forget to discuss their long-term plans, including retirement timelines and how they see their responsibilities evolving over time.

Financial considerations: Bringing on a new partner or team is a financial commitment. You need to assess whether your firm has the resources to support the candidate during the transition and how long it will take for them to contribute meaningfully. Consider how work will transfer—whether it's new work or existing work with or without a pipeline—and what tools, staffing, or case support you need. And, with an abundance of caution, prepare an exit strategy in case the integration doesn't go as planned.

Alignment and transparency: Before finalizing the hire, both you and the new folks should be clear on expectations. Has the firm communicated its requirements for billable hours, revenue generation, and capital contributions? Has it disclosed its compensation structure, benefits, governance model, and strategic plans? Is everyone aligned on the firm's policies on ethics, billing, conflicts, and knowledge management? These conversations ensure alignment and help avoid misunderstandings down the road.

Final checks and client communication: Before the candidate officially joins, confirm all the little details. Ensure that their clients are informed of the transition, they understand the status of their matters, and they are aware of any changes to fee arrangements. Run conflict checks and implement any necessary safeguards. If the candidate will no longer handle certain matters, make sure successor counsel is assigned to ensure continuity and compliance.

Acquirees

If you are joining a firm as part of an acquisition, do your due diligence on that firm. You don't want to move to a firm that isn't aligned with your values or practice, and you certainly don't want to join a sinking ship.

While you can never really know if the grass is greener elsewhere, you should make the effort to learn as much as you can before accepting a position at a new law firm. Below is a list of factors you should explore while doing your homework on your potential new firm. Keep in mind that some may require investigation outside of the interview process, but the extra effort will be worth it if you find something untoward.

Culture

Firm culture can make all the difference between a happy and miserable work environment, so it's worth investigating. Start by asking about the firm's vision and whether its core values have been clearly articulated. It's helpful to know what the firm and its attorneys are proud of and what sets the firm apart from similar firms.

The next step is to dig into the people, especially regarding people who leave. Inquire about recent partner departures and the reasons behind them, as this can reveal internal dynamics. Associate satisfaction is another key indicator—ask how associates feel about the firm and whether there is a pattern of high turnover.

Accessibility and responsiveness of firm leadership are also important, as is clarity around expectations. What are the billable and non-billable requirements for both partners and associates? You'll also want to explore the firm's stance on remote work versus in-office presence, its dress code, and whether attorneys socialize outside of work. These details help paint a picture of the day-to-day environment and overall morale, and whether it's a good fit for you.

Management

Understanding how the firm is governed is as important as understanding its financials. Ask how decisions are made and who sits on the executive or management committee. Clarify which matters are decided by the committee versus a full partner vote and what the voting requirements are for major decisions.

You also want to know who's currently in charge. Identify the firm's key partners and their practice areas, and ask how leadership is selected and developed. If the firm has a tiered partnership structure, find out how many tiers exist, the distinction between equity and non-equity partners, and the criteria for moving between tiers. Find out whether equity partners can be de-equitized, under what circumstances, and who makes that decision. And, if you have long-term aspirations, find out if the firm has a documented succession plan and a written partnership agreement.

Partners and Equity

If being an associate isn't enough, find out how lateral partners are brought into the firm and whether the firm would welcome additional partners or associates as part of the transition. Clarify whether associates have a path to partnership and what input partners have in associate utilization and hiring.

When it comes to compensation, understand how partners are paid and who makes those decisions. Ask how often the compensation structure is reviewed and how origination credit is determined. And what's the buy-in or capital contribution for new equity partners?

Financials

Speaking of payment, let's talk about finances. You don't want to join a firm and find it falling apart underneath you—and the dominant factor in firm stability is often finances. Begin by doing some research using the materials you'll be provided as a potential acquisition. Review performance over the past three to five years, including revenue, profit, and realization rates.

Understand the firm's fee structures—whether they include flat fees, discounts, or contingency matters. And examine the client base: Is it overly reliant on a niche industry or a small number of clients? Are there recession-proof or countercyclical practice areas? And check whether revenue is diversified across partners or concentrated among a few.

Then there's debt. Find out whether the firm holds long-term leases, uses lines of credit, or has any significant financial obligations such as retiring partner buyouts or upcoming capital expenditures. Clarify whether partners are required to personally guarantee firm debt or if credit is used to pay compensation.

You may also want to dig into random financial areas. Is the new firm currently involved in litigation or facing any known liabilities, such as malpractice or discrimination claims? Does the firm maintain key person insurance on any partners? Don't forget about non-equity partners, associates, and staff compensation, as well as how fees from pending contingency matters will be distributed. And, finally, does the firm have any further expansion plans?

Operations

Operations might not be glamorous, but it affects your daily work a lot. If the firm operates ancillary businesses—such as a title company or e-discovery service—ask about ownership, funding, and profit distribution. Inquire whether any partners own the office space and, if so, how rent is determined and whether ownership is open to new partners.

Technology and professional development are also key. Ask about the firm's technology stack, whether attorneys receive an annual marketing budget, and how continuing legal education is handled. Finally, clarify which bar dues the firm covers, including state licenses and voluntary bar associations.

Firm Integration

People often think of mergers as these clean, all-in affairs, but that's rarely the case. When it comes to law firm mergers, it's not uncommon for the process to end up messier than planned. Once two firms start to merge, cultural integration is inevitable, and it happens on multiple levels: staff and leadership.

It costs a lot of money to bring somebody on, and it costs a lot of money to replace someone, whether they're an attorney or a non-attorney employee. Therefore, you want a setup and firm culture that encourages retention of any employees you hire. That all starts with onboarding.

Many law firms don't think much about onboarding. They basically say, "Here's your desk, your computer, and your login. Now, get to work." That's it. There's little to no effort to bring them in culturally, make them feel comfortable, and welcome them into the firm.

The more that a firm spends time thinking through and being intentional about their onboarding process, the more likely success will follow when you hire these people—and the better your chances of retaining them. Part of successful onboarding is being as informative as possible through agreements and handbooks. We will discuss that in the next chapter.

Staff Integration and Turnover

During or after a merger, a loss of people is inevitable. Some leave voluntarily, and some are left behind. Sometimes the acquiring firm doesn't want everybody, or sometimes the people at the firm being acquired don't want to be part of the deal. They might not like the acquiring firm's culture, leadership, or economics.

Conflict analysis is also inevitable, and it's one of the reasons not everybody ends up going along in a merger. An attorney may bring in a big client, but that client may present a direct conflict with a client at the acquiring firm. Now that attorney has a choice: Either give up the client or don't join the new firm.

Those who survive the merger need to feel like they belong in this new, larger firm. You can't have the "new people" feel like they're the freshman class getting hazed. It's more than moving into the same office space; it's about building something new together. Burgeoning relationships and trust among all the new people, from staff to attorneys, is critical.

Leadership Integration and Ego Management

Typically, when two firms come together, you have a head honcho at one firm and a head honcho at the other—or maybe a group of honchos on each side. When you bring them together, you're often dealing with a lot of egos. This is different from cultural integration; it's about *leadership* integration.

Who's going to be where? How do you manage those egos? Someone will need to concede, at least a little; there can't be two chiefs. This is extremely important, and you need to think it through carefully. Ideally, you structure the leadership in a way that sets up the merged firm for success. It's better to go in with a plan than to end up with a huge fight after the fact.

Podcast Feature: Ben Mathis on Adding New Teams or Offices

Not every merger means sharing the same space. On *Founding Partner Podcast*, I interviewed Ben Mathis of Freeman, Mathis & Gary (FMG). He and his firm have grown from eight lawyers in one office to over four hundred lawyers in over thirty offices throughout the country. This is no easy feat, and it has included starting a lot of new offices from scratch as well as acquiring and converting existing firms and practice groups. Ben had some excellent advice on how to handle the expansion.

Invest in Infrastructure

According to Ben, adding new lawyers or offices without back-end support is a recipe for failure. Early on, FMG tried to expand without professional management, and it led to inefficiencies and chaos. "You've got to invest," he told me on the podcast. "You've got to have the infrastructure in place to be able to successfully assimilate." They eventually brought in experienced business professionals (from outside the legal field) to build scalable systems.

Formal Integration Matters

FMG has a structured and comprehensive onboarding process for new teams. This includes in-person visits from human resources (HR), information technology (IT), legal ops, and leadership. "You don't just hire somebody and change the sign," he told me. "Our teams are on-site during the first week, and then we follow up with mentorship and internal training." Each new group gets the hands-on support they need to get up to speed with firm systems, billing, culture, and client expectations.

Define and Defend Your Culture

When evaluating potential acquisitions, Ben looks for alignment with FMG's cultural components: teamwork, excellence, opportunity, and consistency. His firm's values shape how they assess everything from billing practices to collaboration habits.

"We guard our culture zealously," he told me. This means that Ben isn't onboarding just anybody. "Occasionally we have people who say they want to be part of a team," he said. "What they really want to do is be part of a large organization that has a lot of resources, and they want to be left alone, do what they want to do the way they want to do it, and they'll call you if they need anything. Those people do not last."

Timing Is Critical

Ben is deliberate about when to bring new groups onboard. He prefers deals to close in early January to avoid cash flow imbalances caused by onboarding costs and revenue lags. Bringing on a team midyear often means several months of expenses before any meaningful revenue comes in. "By August 1st, it's very difficult to bring on a group and not lose money by year end," he told me.

Know What You're Getting

Ben has learned to go beyond resumes and reputations. When evaluating potential partners or teams, he looks at past employee turnover, firm culture, and leadership style to spot red flags. "A lot of mistakes happen when you know someone socially or through the bar, but haven't looked closely at how they actually run their firm," he explained.

The Risks of a Merger

I can't talk about mergers without talking about risk. Mergers, much like marriages, involve a lot of risks. They are a huge investment, and there are steps you can take to protect that investment. But even the best-laid plans can fail, and that's a possibility you need to be aware of before pressing on with a merger.

Time and Financial Investment

Mergers take a lot of time and money. This is a real financial investment, and it might take a while to pay off. Both sides must be aware of that up front.

The actual costs of a merger depend on the firms involved. But a survey by EY Parthenon (an Ernst and Young subsidiary) found that a merger can cost companies up to 7 percent of the value of the transaction.[9] That can be an extremely significant sum.

Why such a high price tag? There are all sorts of things to consider. For instance, you might need new office space, furniture, and supplies. You might have to pay a third-party vendor to download client files, upload them, and ensure they fit into the new system. None of that is cheap. But beyond that, you have the loss of manpower and productivity. People are packing boxes, moving, and not doing productive client work.

Often, law firm owners don't think through these details early enough. They see the shiny end result and assume everything will fall into place. But moving, training, learning new systems, and managing these logistical issues cost money and slow things down before they start earning.

---

9   "Are You Giving M&A Integration Costs the Attention They Deserve?" EY (the website for Ernst & Young), accessed June 19, 2025, https://www.ey.com/content/dam/ey-unified-site/ey-com/en-cn/insights/strategy-transactions/documents/ey-integration-costs-mergers-and-acquisitions.pdf.

Mistakes During the Move

Then there's the risk factor. When everyone's focused on all the integration work, other risks can arise. Client matters might get mishandled. Personality clashes could create problems. Unknown liabilities might be lurking beneath the surface that could rear their ugly heads later.

Let's say you have a malpractice case at one firm that you don't know about, and despite your best efforts, it suddenly comes over to the new firm. You just bought a lawsuit. Or maybe there are internal issues among attorneys or staff, like sexual harassment claims, that are lurking beneath the surface. These hidden liabilities can be a real problem, so it's crucial to keep an eye out for these baseline risks throughout the process. There are ways to distance yourself from these risks—structuring the deal in a strategic manner, risk-shifting provisions, and insurance paramount among them—but nothing is foolproof.

Worst-Case Scenario: The Failed Merger

Not every merger is a success. A small firm I know of merged into another, larger group. The motivation was fairly typical: The smaller firm was tired of dealing with the administrative overhead—HR, payroll, IT, insurance, compliance, the whole mess. They therefore decided to merge into a more established firm where someone else could handle the logistics, and they could focus on practicing law. (If they had read chapter 1 of this book, they may not have started a firm in the first place. But I digress.)

Unfortunately, handing off the logistics didn't relieve their problems. Cultural disagreements followed, devolving into chaos. Personalities didn't click, expectations didn't align, and the whole thing began to unravel.

After about eighteen months, it was obvious the merger wasn't working. So what did they do? They ended up splitting again. They "unmerged." Which, as you can imagine, was a huge pain and not without drama. Allegations of wrongdoing flew around—none of them true, but the kind of mess that bubbles up when business relationships fracture.

Worst of all, each firm had to go back to their clients and say, "Hey, remember when we moved to this new firm? Well, now we're moving again." Clients were understandably asking, "What in the world is going on?" Some of them left, not wanting to deal with the confusion.

As you can see, a failed merger can be a disaster for everyone involved. You lose credibility, time, and money. These aren't short-term decisions; you're tying your brand and your reputation to someone else's ship, and failure is a possibility you'll need to reconcile with before moving forward.

Merging into Something New

Naturally, we had to run conflicts. There were lots of discussions over several months. We looked at numbers, compensation systems, all of that. We had many meetings to see if things fit personality-wise. For a while, it felt like a good move, so we did it.

Before I could bring my clients over, we had to run conflict checks to make sure there were no issues. Once that was cleared, I had to notify my clients—let them know I was leaving and going to a new firm, and ask them if they wanted to come with me. Then came the logistical transition of getting me, my files, and my clients into the new firm's systems—documents, pleadings, filings, everything. That took time. Even after I joined, it took time to get fully up and running.

Whether you're trying to keep your law firm solvent or are looking to expand, a merger can be a great way to evolve your firm into the next stage of the law firm life cycle. With proper planning and consideration of the risks, a merger can be a big win for your team, your clients, and the leader—you.

9. TRANSITION

"I'll just die at my desk." This is a line I hear far too often, and not as a joke. For many lawyers, death is the default succession plan. No road map, no transition. And somehow, attorneys wear this lack of a plan like a badge of honor.

I don't think it's a badge of honor. I think it's the worst succession plan out there.

If you're anything like my clients, you might be thinking, *Succession planning? Who cares? I'll shut my firm down when I'm ready.* That's the attitude of many law firm owners. But you *should* care, especially if you don't want your firm to close its doors after you retire.

If you don't want to shut down, it's time to think about transitioning—bringing in the next generation or two and setting the stage for retirement. Neglecting this part of the firm journey means setting up yourself and the firm for disaster. With early succession planning, though, your firm can live a long, happy life after you've stepped down.

In this chapter, we will explore why a succession plan is so critical, when you need to put one in place, and what two components comprise a strong succession plan.

The Cost of Not Having a Succession Plan

Succession planning is a cornerstone of any successful business, but a lot of small law firms don't want to touch it. A succession plan is a lot like a will: You have more control if you have one, and without one, you can inadvertently leave a real mess. If you decide to ignore it and keep plugging along, four big issues can arise: (1) the early demise of your firm, (2) an unpleasant generational divide within your firm, (3) the loss of your considerable investment (your life's work), and (4) the harm it can cause to others, including estate complications.

It Can Kill Your Firm Early

That's right. Succession planning isn't only about what happens after you retire; it affects your firm years before that. A lack of planning can destabilize a once-thriving practice long before the founding partners step away. Here's what happens when law firm owners delay succession planning:

- Younger attorneys see no path forward. If there's no plan—or if the plan hasn't been clearly communicated—your top associates and junior partners will assume there's no future for them, so they leave.

- The talent gap widens. As strong attorneys exit, the gap between leadership and the next generation grows, which makes it harder to recruit experienced replacements.

- Profitability takes a hit. Without seasoned attorneys, firms are forced to repeatedly hire and train less experienced lawyers, and that turnover is expensive.

- Current or prospective clients start to worry. They may wonder whether you'll be with them through the end of their matters, and they may opt to leave.

- Firm value declines. High turnover and lower profitability reduce the firm's overall value at a time when owners are hoping to cash out or slow down.

I've seen this time and time again, and I have begun taking precautions to keep it from happening in my own law firm. I think a lot about what I'm building; I'm not one of those lawyers who ignores it. I want this firm to grow, not only for growth's sake but for younger lawyers to stick around when they see real opportunities to advance.

Growth creates those opportunities, so Law Firm GC is expanding deliberately and strategically. That's how you give talented people room to rise and eventually take over. Let them see you expanding and thriving so they know that, eventually, someone will need to take your place. That's the opposite of killing your firm early.

It Can Cause a Generational Divide

I noted above that a firm without a succession plan creates a generational ceiling. The second or third generation of attorneys bump up against it, unable to move into leadership roles. Frustrated, they leave—often taking their books of business with them. Others see the exodus and follow suit.

What's left is a top-heavy firm with a widening gap in the middle. It ends up like a Jenga tower with too many pieces pulled from the center—unstable and at risk of collapse.

The thing is, even when those younger attorneys leave to join other firms, they often find the same problem waiting for them. Unless someone breaks the cycle, it repeats. Would you like to be the one to break it? Doing so can help you build an incredibly talented and loyal attorney staff.

It Can Sink Your Life's Work

If you're a lawyer, you've probably poured your heart and soul into your firm. Maybe you took out a mortgage or borrowed from your retirement to get started. You've invested everything. You've thought through every detail—office space (or none at all), staffing, team benefits, marketing, experts, trials. You've paid attention to it all.

And yet, somehow, the one thing that gets skipped is the plan for what happens if something unexpected happens. Or how the firm passes to the next generation.

You spend your entire career building your practice. You've spent—and are still spending—your time, energy, and money to build your firm. Why wouldn't you close the last loophole and protect your investment?

Do the hard work and figure out how to pass it to another generation. Hiring your replacement is an investment in the future. Don't be scared to do it. Taking the time to think through and devise a transition plan for your law practice is worth the investment.

It Can Harm Others

In the 2010s, there was a successful solo practitioner in his late thirties whose practice was consistently generating seven figures in fees. He had a couple of part-time attorneys who helped out, and his wife, who wasn't a lawyer, managed the office. They had five young kids and were on top of the world.

Then one night, on his way home from work, this attorney was killed in a car accident. In an instant, his family's sole source of income came to a screeching halt. To make things worse, he didn't have any life insurance.

He also didn't have a succession plan.

Because there was no succession plan, almost all the value he had built in his firm vanished. His team was left scrambling to find homes for his clients to make sure their matters were protected, and then the firm folded. Whatever value the family received? You would have to call it liquidation value.

It's a terrible thing to think about, but life is unpredictable. It's better to have a plan in place than to leave it up to chance. Think of how many people would be affected if something like this were to happen to you—not only your family and friends, but your staff and clients as well.

A succession plan protects your clients if you're suddenly incapacitated. A well-structured backup plan helps ensure deadlines, court dates, etc. are adhered to. If appropriate, client funds and property held in trust can be more expeditiously returned to clients.

You also want to minimize the risk of claims or liability against you or your estate. With a plan in place, you will prevent an inadvertent lapse in insurance coverage. An organized practice and a designated backup attorney can prevent any malpractice that might occur within a transition period. This is important because death or disability isn't a defense to a malpractice claim. Your estate could be on the hook for something like that—but the chances lessen if you plan ahead.

When to Start Succession Planning

I hope I've convinced you that you need a succession plan. You may be asking yourself when you should start.

When is the best time to plant a tree? Twenty years ago. When is the second-best time? Today. It's the same with succession planning. The sooner you start, the better off you—and your firm—will be. Too many lawyers wait until it's too late. And the truth is, the shorter your timeline to transition or exit, the harder it is to pull off a solid plan.

Law firm succession planning isn't optional or something you can put off until you're "ready." There's an event horizon, and once you cross it, it's often too late to escape the consequences. The firm starts to unravel, and the damage is hard to reverse. This means it's best to get started as soon as possible. Even if you think you've got twenty years left in your career, start now. Sketch out a plan. Think it through. Waiting only makes it harder.

At a minimum, if you want to get real value out of your practice, give yourself time—ideally at least two to five years—to put a plan in place before your potential retirement. Succession planning is a process, not a one-time event, and it takes that long to complete. Allotting up to five years gives you space to clean up your personal finances, organize your firm, boost its value, and identify the right buyer. It can be completed faster, but the results are rarely optimal.

Additionally, like a will, succession planning isn't something you do once and then forget. It requires consistent, thoughtful attention because circumstances change. If you don't make succession a firm priority and revisit your plan regularly, you risk facing the very problems that cause instability—like generational divides and leadership gaps—and ultimately lead to the decline of your firm.

The Planned Transition/Sale

Many lawyers don't believe that a law firm can be sold. That isn't true. But admittedly, a third-party sale isn't easy. I've handled purchases and sales of law firms and have had the pleasure of interviewing several lawyers on *Founding Partner Podcast* who have sold their firms. Firms with high-volume practices approach succession differently than smaller, more focused firms. True solos with no associates have fewer options than those who've built teams. And if you already have equity partners, succession planning is usually addressed in your partnership agreement (hopefully in writing, like I suggested in chapter 2).

With all that in mind, assuming you're not looking to shut down, you can go about a planned transition in a few ways: an internal sale, external sale, or merger / of counsel.

Podcast Feature: Patrick Slaughter on Internal Transition

Patrick Slaughter had a small family law practice in Knoxville, Tennessee, and he was able to sell his practice to an external buyer and walk away right after closing. Today, he works with law firm owners to help them build lucrative and fulfilling law practices. On *Founding Partner Podcast*, he explained to me how he was able to pull off his own sale.

Perhaps the most important factor for Patrick was leading an independent firm. Having successfully run the firm from Florida while it operated in Tennessee, he could easily show that the business wasn't owner-dependent. This meant he had to delegate—something most lawyers shy away from.

"Lawyers have got to stop wearing twenty hats," he told me. "It amazes me when a lawyer will decide to spend a half a day working on their website. I can find somebody to manage a website for two hundred dollars an hour at most, but I can bill at four or five hundred dollars an hour myself. It would make more sense for me to spend my time doing things that I can build at four hundred dollars and paying somebody less to do something."

This echoes a basic tenet of scaling—you can't do it all yourself—which also makes your business more appealing to buyers. "You don't want to wear the cheap hats," Patrick reminds me. "You want to wear the hat that makes the most money and pay the other people with the cheap hats to do the job."

Creating an Independent Business

From the beginning, Patrick prioritized systems and operations that didn't require his presence. This meant a digitized policies and procedures manual and templated legal pleadings with command logic for auto-population, which allowed for easier onboarding of clients and new hires.

"I realized I needed to have everything done for them so I can just plug them in, kind of like what McDonald's does with their new fry cooks," he explained in regards to onboarding new clients and staff members. "So we had all of our pleadings already digitized, using different kinds of command logic so they auto-populated."

Patrick has always been ahead of the curve, using virtual tools like Zoom and HelloSign before the COVID-19 pandemic and implementing customer relationship management integration like Clio Grow for lead and client management. He told me a great story about when he realized the value of the latter for freeing up his time and, eventually, making his law firm more valuable. It also set him up for success during the pandemic. While the world was struggling to onboard all these digital tools, he had already done the legwork:

> One summer in 2018, my family and I were driving down to Florida for a three-week vacation when I got a call from this guy named Tony that I'll never forget. He said, "I really want to hire you for this juvenile court case I have tomorrow."
>
> I told Tony, "Well, I ain't going to be there tomorrow. I'm going to Florida."
>
> He asked, "You got anybody who works for you?"
>
> I said, "Yeah, I got some associates." In the passenger seat, my wife, Zena, checks the calendar and confirms a slot. "We have eight o'clock a.m. availability. But

I don't know how we're going to do this. You've got to sign a fee agreement and pay me, and I can't take your money until you sign the agreement. My staff in Tennessee can't sign for me, so I don't know how that's going to work."

Then Zena says, "What about that HelloSign stuff?"

I think, *Well, I guess we could try this crap that I got that I don't know how to use.* I pulled over at a rest area and said to Tony, "Let's see if we can figure this out. I might be able to send you this PDF, and you can sign it electronically. Then you can pay us with a credit card, and maybe I can get my associate Luke to go to your hearing."

Tony was happy with that. My fee agreement was already uploaded as part of the onboarding with Lexicata. Zena figured it out; sent Tony the contract. He signed it, sent it back, and paid the trust deposit by credit card. Luke was at Tony's hearing the next day and got him what he wanted.

It was the darndest thing I'd ever seen. At that minute, I realized—instantaneously—that I was free.

Before, I used to tell people the only reason I had an office was so I could have a conference room. I'd do a consultation on the phone, then they'd schedule a time to come in. I'd go over the same crap I just talked to them about anyway, but they'd bring me a check, we'd sign the fee agreement, and then we'd go on.

But with this, suddenly I realized I didn't have to do in-person consultations anymore. I didn't have to meet with people, which was shocking to me. I thought people would want to meet me because they're trusting me with their retirement plans or kids or life, but they didn't care.

We were one of the first firms ever to start doing consultations that way. At that point, I realized there was no reason to have anybody in the office except maybe for depositions. So we started doing that. We started doing our consults strictly by phone and Zoom. Everything—the whole retaining process—was electronic.

Obviously, law firms like this are now more common than they were before the pandemic. But would you be able to do what Patrick did—pull over at a rest stop and onboard a client in another state? If you can, not only is your time freed up but your firm is also suddenly worth a lot more.

Patrick also used digital, comprehensive financial records. This helped him stay profitable while he ran the business, and it also gave him a huge boost in the value of his firm when it was time to sell. The digital numbers demonstrated consistent six-figure monthly cash flow, supported by proper documentation and historical data, and this skyrocketed the firm's value. He also used payroll instead of K-1s, making the firm more attractive to Small Business Administration (SBA) lenders.

"We gave [our records] to the lender on the same day he requested the materials, and he was shocked," Patrick said. "He came back and he told us, 'This firm is worth seven figure plus,' and I about fell over. Everybody else had told me it wasn't worth anything, and I'd been willing to sell it for a whole lot less than that."

Other Factors: Marketing, Awards, and Sales Structure

In addition to creating a well-documented, digital business that could run without him, Patrick created over seventy Q and A–style videos on YouTube, providing a lasting digital footprint and ongoing lead generation. He also built authority through awards, reviews, and recognitions that added brand value.

Patrick worked with a buyer who secured funding through the SBA, aided by the firm's sound structure and profitability. He sold his firm assets rather than corporate stock, reducing complexity and retaining the business entity. He also negotiated a clean break, selling the firm without being required to stay on for a transition period. "He gave me the money on April 18th, and I was gone on April 19th," he told me. And although he didn't inform staff until the sale was finalized, the structure in place enabled a smooth transfer of responsibilities.

Buy-In for New Members

An important distinction exists between starting a partnership and expanding one. When founding a firm with one or more partners, it's assumed that all parties will contribute, financially and otherwise, from the outset. When a new partner is brought into an existing firm, however, the issue of "buy-in" becomes central. This refers to the new partner's financial contribution, which should reflect their equity share and stake in the firm's success.

Although buy-in is a given when forming a firm together, its implications and mechanics need to be revisited when growth or succession is on the table. Many firms eventually reach a point where they consider offering equity to a senior associate. That's when questions around valuation, compensation models, and long-term commitments become especially pressing.

In this scenario, should you have to buy your equity, or should it be given to you? There are two schools of thought. Most people, including me, would say that you have to buy in. Others may argue that you've earned it over time. Make sure to consider this and create a policy that works for you.

Podcast Feature: Jessica Stern on Preemptive Steps Toward a Future Sale

Most lawyers don't consider selling their law firms until they're thinking about retiring. But by then, it's often too late to build something someone else wants to buy.

On *Founding Partner Podcast*, I interviewed former criminal immigration law firm owner Jessica Stern. She built a highly focused firm in the "crimmigration" space, scaled it to fifteen team members, and ultimately sold it to a third-party buyer.

Not many lawyers pull that off. Even fewer do it on their own terms. Here's how Jessica planned ahead and reaped the benefits.

Specialization builds value: A focused practice helps clients find you, makes marketing clearer, and positions you as a category expert. Jessica's niche was a competitive advantage. "I was able to see the niche of criminal and immigration. . . . Nobody was doing it, and our clients needed it," she told me. "I saw a way to do it differently, and I took the leap."

Your firm should be able to function without you: Jessica developed systems and hired intentionally so she wasn't the center of the business. "You have to rely on the fact that you've run your firm in a way that was sustainable for you and was profitable for you, and therefore it will continue to be sustainable and profitable for the next owner," she said. That efficiency was critical when it came time to step away.

Track what matters: You need clean data for any business sale. For a law firm, that means leads, revenue, client outcomes, marketing spend, and conversion rates. When a buyer asked, Jessica could *show*—not just *tell*—her business success. "Thankfully, I had the most amazing bookkeeper who gave me the confidence and the information that I needed in beautiful financial reports," she told me.

Build with the end in mind: Even if you're not planning to sell, ask yourself if your firm is something someone could buy. That standard will push you to build a better business. Jessica said, "That's important to be thinking through well before you would go to sell a firm, because if it wasn't really working for you, then why would it work for someone else?"

Don't wait until you're burned out: Jessica made the choice to exit while her firm was still growing. "I just wasn't consistently having fun anymore," she said. "On paper, it probably was crazy to sell it because it really was consistently profitable. There was a formula that was working, but I was tired of how it was working." Her firm's strong position and her own clarity gave her leverage and space to move into something new.

You don't need a massive firm or a sales team to learn from Jessica's success story. You need to shift how you think. Act like an owner, not just a lawyer. Because whether you sell, scale, or stay put, that mindset will help you build something worth keeping or passing on.

Internal Sale Versus External Sale

One common approach in law firm succession planning is the internal transition. This can take the form of a gradual sale of equity over time, or it can be a one-time sale of all equity.

The key is having a lawyer at your firm who can buy you out and take over. If you don't have a strong candidate currently, you'll need to find one and bring them in. That can take time, so if this is your preferred plan, don't wait too long to find a good prospect.

As for external sales, most jurisdictions have adopted the American Bar Association Model Rules of Professional Conduct that allow for the external sale of a law practice. While the details vary by jurisdiction, the core requirements are fairly consistent. One of the most important aspects of this is the client disclosure requirement. If you're looking to sell externally, you must inform your clients of your intention to sell, obtain their permission to share their information with potential buyers, and remind them that they are free to hire another lawyer instead of the purchaser.

This process can understandably create anxiety. Clients may get nervous and leave before the sale is complete—and if the transaction falls through, you may find yourself with fewer clients than when you started. You'll need to think carefully about timing and how to approach your clients during this period.

What Is Your Firm Worth? Planning for the Sale

Do you know what your firm is worth? Some lawyers assume their firm isn't worth anything. Others know there's value there, but they're not sure how much.

If you've been hoping to potentially sell your firm at some point, the price you can garner depends on a lot of factors that are specific to your practice. Here are some of the details that impact valuation:

- What kind of practice do you have? Is it high volume with lower-value cases, low volume but big trial wins, or somewhere in between?
- What's the present-day expected value of your active cases?
- How strong is your brand or reputation in the market?
- How much of the market do you serve?
- Where is your firm located?
- What assets do you have? (Such as your team, your digital presence, or any trademarks.)
- Is your practice area growing or shrinking?

Finally, here's a big one: The less your firm depends on you, the more it's worth. If you're doing everything yourself—running operations, handling finances, managing marketing, doing the legal work—your firm's value will likely be lower. If you've built a team and systems that run without you, buyers will see real value there. This is another reason why building good systems and processes, and hiring a team well-versed in those systems and processes, is so crucial. You can find a list of ideas on ways to increase the value of your law firm on the resources page here: https://www.lawfirm gc.com/life-cycle-resources/.

Structuring the Sale

When selling a law firm, the same major issues always come up, and they need to be addressed carefully in any law firm sale or transition. I've listed the ones I've seen frequently. Beyond these core elements, every deal will have its own unique terms depending on the specifics of the firm, the goals of the parties involved, and the specifics of the structure of the sale.

Method and Details of Payment

When you're selling a law firm, the first question is simple: What's the price? But the buyer's method of payment matters nearly as much as the price itself. Will they produce a lump sum up-front? Or are there payment terms stretched out over time?

Within those terms, there's more to unpack. For instance, how is the deal being financed? Is a bank involved? Or is it seller-financed, meaning the buyer signs a promissory note agreeing to pay the seller in installments over time? Sometimes the payments are even tied to future revenue targets, so the seller only gets paid if the firm hits certain financial goals after the sale. Any deal needs to clearly address these structural elements.

Post-Sale Seller Involvement (or Lack Thereof)

Another key consideration is whether the seller is staying on with the firm after the sale or walking away immediately. For example, in the case of my podcast guest Patrick Slaughter, the seller closed the deal and exited the same day, never to return. But more often, the buyer wants the seller to stay on for a transition period. This helps clients feel confident continuing with the firm and assists the staff in smoothly transitioning to new ownership. Without that bridge, there's a risk that clients or staff may leave shortly after the sale.

Sometimes, the seller themselves may want to stay involved. They may no longer want to manage the business, but they still enjoy practicing law. In that case, a post-sale role tailored to their preferences can be a win for both sides. The former firm owner can continue doing what they love while the buyer benefits from their ongoing experience and relationships.

Restrictive Covenants

Another important issue to think through is restrictive covenants, particularly non-competes. Generally, non competes for lawyers are considered unethical and unenforceable. But there is a key exception: in the context of selling a law practice. I won't buy a firm without a restrictive covenant in the agreement. The last thing I want as a buyer is to have the seller open up shop down the street the next day, telling all their former clients, "I'm back—come see me here." Without a non compete tied to the sale, what I purchased could walk right out the door.

Merger / Of Counsel

The last path in law firm succession is for the firm owner to join another firm like we talked about in the last chapter—often under a merger or of counsel arrangement. This can be a win-win when combined with succession. You get to gradually step back from the day-to-day while still transitioning your clients over time. Often, you can strike a deal for residual payments for bringing in new clients, continuing work on active files, training younger lawyers, and more.

This is a common approach I've seen work well for solo practices or solely owned firms. The "retiring" attorney associates with another existing firm and begins transitioning clients to the new firm. In return, the new firm agrees to pay the retiring lawyer a percentage of any new dollars that come in the door from the retiring lawyer's original clients even if the retiring lawyer doesn't work on the new matters. This setup allows the retiring lawyer to wind down their daily legal tasks while still monetizing their client relationships.

A merger or of counsel relationship like this also aligns the interests of the retiring lawyer and the new firm. The new firm only pays for new dollars in the door, and the retiring lawyer is incentivized to transition existing clients or even bring in new clients. The new firm gets a new revenue stream while you get a residual "retirement payout" and the clients find a new home. This is a much better outcome than shutting down the practice.

Preparing for Your Next Phase

A lot of lawyers say they want to step away from practice, but you can't always take that at face value. Many find that they can't retire, either for financial reasons or because they have no idea what to do with themselves. Here's what you can do right now to make sure you're ready when the time comes.

Can You Afford to Retire?

A lot of lawyers can't leave the profession, not because they don't want to, but because they haven't saved enough. They spent everything they earned, and when it comes time to retire, they can't afford to step down.

It's unbelievably common for attorneys to live at or even above their means. Many lawyers believe that keeping up appearances is part of the profession—the tailored clothing, expensive watch, upscale vehicle, country club membership, and fancy office are absolute necessities in their minds. When it all catches up, you're not left with much. I've talked to divorce lawyers who have represented high-powered partners at major firms—people making a million dollars a year—and some of them are flat-out in the red.

Honestly, there's no magic fix for this problem. If you're out of money and still need income, you'll probably have to keep working. But my advice is to think about this as early as you can, deciding what you need (and don't need), and figuring out how to get it. I've always tried to build my life around optionality. I want choices. I want to be able to work because I choose to, not because I must. That means living beneath my means. Saving consistently. Building a life and practice that give me some financial breathing room.

If you have five, ten, or twenty years, or even multiple decades before you want to retire, start planning now. Or maybe you love practicing law and never want to stop. That's great. But let that be your decision—not something forced on you because of poor planning.

Build a Multifaceted Life

Before law school, I was a huge reader. I would read for pleasure all the time. Then I went to law school, started practicing, and didn't read a single book for fun for at least fifteen years. I was so burned out from reading case law and legal memos that the idea of picking up a novel felt exhausting. Can you relate to that? Maybe not for reading, but for something else?

The law can take everything if you let it, so be intentional about not letting it. Design a life that leaves room for more. Build an identity that's not just tied to being a lawyer. Have friends outside the legal world. Pursue hobbies. Create other interests. It's better for your health, it helps manage stress, and it gives you something richer to hold on to when the time comes to step back.

This is incredibly hard for a lot of lawyers, but you've got to carve out the time and the mental space to do this, especially if retirement is just around the corner. It may not feel natural at first, but if you give yourself permission, most people find that they want to do something more than the next case or the next deal.

What's Next for You?

Building a multifaceted identity can go a long way toward helping you decide what to do once you retire, but it isn't enough. Unless you know what's next, it's easy to stay stuck, paralyzed by uncertainty and caught between wanting change and fearing the unknown.

To snap out of that mindset, spend time reflecting deeply on what you want your life to look like after you step down from your current position. If you don't have something to transition to, it becomes impossible to let go of what you've built.

What's next for you? Are you planning to launch a second career, maybe as a mediator? Do you want to keep practicing but in a reduced role? Or are you ready to step away—spend time with family, travel, play some well-earned rounds of golf? For me, I would love to start a second career as a part-time private concert promoter in my golden years.

Succession is an emotional process as much as it is a legal and business process. As you approach succession, begin to identify yourself as something other than a lawyer. This will help you move from merely thinking about succession to actually achieving it. Whatever your vision is, it matters as much as your vision for the firm did when you were getting started.

So start seeing yourself as something other than "the lawyer who owns the firm." It might feel uncomfortable, but it's a necessary shift if you want to move from *thinking* about succession to actually making it happen. And once you've done that inner work, everything else—plans, timelines, documents—gets a whole lot easier.

The Unpredictable Nature of Law Firm Breakups

I've been through a law firm dissolution from the inside. The dynamics of how that dissolution went down were fascinating, and that experience still helps me today.

Many years ago, I was told in December I would be made partner at the firm in January. At the time, the firm had around twenty-five lawyers and had come off its best year ever. They had a good distribution of originating attorneys across three generations. It looked like they were set to really start growing.

But after the New Year, right after I settled into my new office, a practice group within the firm announced they were leaving to start their own venture. In all, two partners and another four attorneys were leaving along with some staff. It was like a bomb had dropped. I hadn't even attended my first partner meeting yet.

The announcement reverberated through the firm. There were closed-door meetings everywhere. The group that was leaving stayed through the end of January, and things got extremely awkward. I harbored no ill will and wished that group the best on their next venture, but not everyone shared my view.

Eventually, January ended, and the group left. A big swath of the office stood empty. It was weird.

Then, another partner announced he was leaving to go elsewhere. That second announcement spooked some folks. In the wake of the departures, more associates found landing spots and jumped ship. Then the staff got scared and started leaving as well.

The closed-door meetings kept happening as these departures led to everyone thinking about their next move. Did they want to stay and rebuild here, or should they move elsewhere?

It culminated with a partners meeting in May. The agenda was to have a frank discussion and get input from everyone. I walked into the meeting thinking that, as the newest and youngest partner, my opinions wouldn't matter much and wouldn't be asked for.

The meeting began with the managing partner stating that we were there to hear from everyone about what they were going to do. He turned to me and said, "Hawkins, let's start with you."

I wasn't prepared for that. I fumbled for what felt like forever, and then I got the words out. "I don't want to commit to signing another lease," I said. "I'm planning to leave."

We then went around the room from newest to oldest partner. Each partner said something similar to me. When we got to the managing partner, he said the same thing.

I was gone six weeks later, and more left after me. A few partners, attorneys, and staff stayed behind to wind up the firm. By December 31 of that year, the whole firm was gone.

I kept in touch with some who stayed behind, and they told me it was the most depressing time in their career. The office was empty and cavernous. Rooms were filled floor to ceiling with empty three-ring binders that were left as files were destroyed and disposed of. So many people had left, and what had been a vibrant, fun workplace became a crypt.

That surreal experience taught me a lot about how quickly a firm can die. Having a great year is no guarantee that the firm will survive another year.

It was interesting to see how associates and staff lost their nerve and immediately started looking for the exits. I don't blame them. No matter how many years of loyal service they gave to the firm, they had to look after themselves and their families. To keep some or all of them, senior leadership needed to approach them immediately and likely offer retention bonuses. But that didn't happen, and eventually, everyone left.

While this firm broke up because of the exodus of workers, there are many other reasons why a firm might close. Maybe there is no next generation to take over. Maybe the firm never gained traction. Maybe a solo attorney is ready to retire and has no exit strategy other than closure, or a primary client leaves and there isn't enough business or energy to keep the firm going. Whatever the reason, though, someone has to stay behind to shred the files and lock the doors.

Planning for Successful Succession

Let's be honest—succession planning probably isn't at the top of your to-do list. You're busy building your firm, practicing law, and spending any leftover time on family, hobbies, or trying to relax. Thinking about the end? It's not exactly appealing. But don't fall into that trap—make the decision today to put a plan in place.

Succession planning in law firms is hard, but just because it's hard doesn't mean you should ignore it or not try. And trust me—I'm walking the walk here. Succession planning is baked into the DNA of my firm, and it has been from day one. The very name of the practice—Law Firm GC—is a deliberate choice. I went the trade name route in part because I had the end in mind. Like I mentioned in chapter 2, if a firm's brand is tied to one individual's name, the next generation may feel compelled to rebrand when that individual steps away. That erodes value. By using a trade name, I've kept the door open for someone else to step in seamlessly when the time comes.

Law Firm GC won't die with me. My goal is to build something that lasts—an organization future leaders can inherit, improve, and scale in ways I might not be able to imagine today.

When you start thinking about succession, begin with the end in mind. Those who are seeking to transition out must be mentally and emotionally ready to let go. If you're not, succession isn't going to happen. Spend the time to reflect deeply on what you want your life to look like after the transition.

You've built something worth protecting. Now it's time to make sure it thrives today and tomorrow.

10. CLOSE

For everyone, death is inevitable. It's also usually inevitable in the law firm life cycle, even with succession planning. I have a rule of thumb on the maximum lifespan of a law firm: thirty-five years, or within five years of the departure of the last founding partner.

The vast majority of law firms end up shutting down eventually. This is the phase of the law firm life cycle I hope my own firm never has to go through, but it happens all the time. I've helped a firm close its doors after being in existence for 120-something years. There are other firms that close within a year.

Whether you've decided a succession plan isn't for you or things aren't working out, shutting down a law firm isn't as simple as turning off the lights and locking the doors, especially for a firm that has been in existence for a long time. There are client files, furniture, vendors, landlords, trust accounts, and much more to deal with. This takes time, energy, and money to do. And someone has to do it. This final chapter, therefore, will be dedicated to the end of the law firm life cycle.

The Emergency Backup Plan

There are two basic levels to succession planning. In the last chapter, we talked about a planned succession. Here, I want to talk about an emergency backup plan, otherwise known as the "hit by a bus" plan. This plan kicks into gear if you're suddenly unable to continue working because of death, injury, or some other unforeseen factor. Every solo or small firm owner needs one of these, and they consist of three steps.

1. Organize Your Practice

First, you need to get your practice in a minimally organized state. Hopefully, your filing system doesn't consist of papers stacked around your office and organized in a way that only you understand. If your firm isn't already primarily digital, you need to get it there. Creating good systems and processes like we discussed in chapter 4 will help tremendously with this step.

As part of the organization process, pull together and document the "who, what, where, and how" of certain essential elements of your practice. For example, if someone had to step into your practice today, could they easily generate a list of your active client matters and find client contact information? The "who, what, where, and how" can guide someone through this difficult process should the need arise.

2. Designate a Backup Attorney

Second, you will need to designate a backup attorney. This lawyer will parachute in and triage your practice if you are suddenly unable to continue. Unless your spouse or heir is a lawyer, they can't serve in this role.

Your backup attorney, like the executor of your will, needs to be informed of their newfound position. So once you've picked a lawyer who you would like as your backup attorney, have a conversation with them. Discuss this plan with them, show them around your office, and execute agreements and related documentation. Don't let them get blindsided if the worst should occur.

Oftentimes, two lawyers reciprocate and agree to serve as backup attorneys for each other. In some states, you're asked to list your backup attorney with the state bar. In that case, it is especially imperative to make sure the lawyer you are listing is aware of their status as your backup lawyer. I've heard stories of lawyers getting called by the state bar and, to their surprise, being told they were designated as a backup attorney for someone. That isn't how you want to ask someone to fill this role for you.

3. Set Up Short-Term Funding

Third, you should put some source of emergency short-term funding in place to finance the transition of your practice.

Landlords, vendors, and employees still need to be paid. Tail coverage will need to be purchased. Serving as a backup attorney can be a substantial task and should be compensated as well. There are affordable insurance products you can use for this (like key person life insurance, business overhead expense insurance, and others), or you can create a reserve fund for this purpose.

Closing Your Law Practice

I have a detailed checklist of twenty-six steps for closing a law firm, but as I'm not looking to bore you, I've distilled it into the general areas you'll want to look at if you decide it's time to close. For the full checklist, please visit https://www.lawfirmgc.com/life-cycle-resources/.

Client and Case Management

Closing a law practice begins with understanding your obligations to your clients and to any partners or co-owners. You'll need to have someone review your firm's foundational documents to identify any procedural requirements. Then, a comprehensive client list and inventory of all files must be created, distinguishing between active and inactive matters.

As you look at the work that's left, prioritize urgent deadlines by reviewing calendars and case files. Have your assistant stay on top of all communications, including unopened mail, email, and voicemail. After all, just because you're closing doesn't mean you're already closed.

Most importantly, reach out to clients with active matters. Whether you're transferring files to another attorney or helping clients find new counsel, clear communication and written consent are so important during this phase. Clients need to know what's happening, what their options are, and what steps they need to take to protect their interests.

File Handling

Managing client files is one of the most sensitive and time-consuming parts of closing a practice. I advise my clients to start by having their staff make copies of all files for clients while retaining originals for your records. Every file transfer should be documented, with signed receipts and clear records of what was returned and to whom.

Take special care with original documents. Wills, titles, and other irreplaceable items must be returned to clients and never destroyed.

For closed files, follow your jurisdiction's retention rules. Files that can't be returned or destroyed must be preserved under the care of an authorized custodian. Clients should also be informed about where their closed files will be stored and how they can retrieve them in the future. Accuracy and diligence here are vital for your own protection as well as your clients' security.

Insurance and Compliance

Before winding down operations, contact your malpractice insurance provider to discuss tail coverage, which protects you from claims that may arise after the firm closes. Review all other business insurance policies and cancel those that are no longer needed.

If you're withdrawing from active cases, ensure that either a Substitution of Attorney is filed or a motion to withdraw is granted by the court. These steps are essential to maintaining ethical and professional standards during the transition.

Business Operations

The business side of closing a firm involves an exhaustive and exhausting list of practical tasks. Have your assistant notify your payroll provider, landlord, and vendors. Someone will need to review your office for uncashed checks or undeposited funds, then determine whether they should be returned or processed.

You and your staff will also need to finalize billing, collect outstanding receivables, and resolve any fee disputes; coordinate the return or transfer of client trust funds and begin terminating leases and vendor contracts; and close all credit cards, lines of credit, and business bank accounts.

Trust Account

Reconciling your trust account is a nonnegotiable step from a legal standpoint. Every dollar must be accounted for and properly disbursed. Work closely with your bookkeeper or certified public accountant to ensure that all client funds are returned or transferred according to their instructions. This is one of the most scrutinized aspects of closing a practice, so pay special attention.

Assets and Retirement

If your firm has a retirement plan, notify the plan administrator and coordinate the transition of any accounts. You'll also need to decide what to do with office furniture, equipment, and other assets. Are you selling, donating, or storing them? Make sure everything is accounted for and properly handled.

Communications and Digital Presence

Even after the doors close, your firm may linger online and in public directories. Plan to shut down your website and social media accounts within a year, or leave a simple landing page with updated contact information. If possible, forward your office phone number for around a year to ensure clients and colleagues can still reach you.

The End of an Era

When I was in high school, I was the drummer in a rock and roll band, and we wanted to be rock stars. We wrote original songs and had big dreams. Music was everything to me back then. I almost didn't go to college because I was so convinced I was going to make it in music.

I remember telling my dad that I planned to skip college and chase the dream. He didn't take it well.

"That would be the biggest mistake of your life," he said.

"I don't care," I replied. "I'm doing it."

"If that's your decision, you'll be on your own," he said. "No financial support, no help, nothing." He crossed his arms and nodded to himself. "You'll need to return everything your mother and I have ever given you, too, including the clothes on your back."

I dug in my heels. "I can do it without anyone's help," I insisted, though I kept my clothes on. Within two weeks, reality sank in, and I knew college was for me.

I tell that story not because I regret choosing college over music, but because that love for music never went away. I gave up the dream of being a drummer, but not the connection to that creative part of myself. And now, as I look ahead to life after law, I know exactly what I want to do next.

But first, I will have to do something about my firm. As we learned in this chapter, there are two ways the life cycle of a law firm can end: succession (evolution into something new) or closure. For Law Firm GC, I hope closure doesn't come for many decades after I step down. But if you're planning on shutting down operations before you retire, closing your firm the right way is essential if you want to avoid trouble with clients, creditors, your staff, or the law.

So take a leaf out of my book and treat your succession plan like you would any important client matter. Block time on your calendar. Set real deadlines for each milestone. Write down your plan. Stick to it. Follow through.

You have to do this because shutting down a law firm takes time. It costs money. And no—you can't simply turn off the lights and walk away. If you're around to handle it yourself, great. But if you're not, someone else will have to. And in that case, you'll need two things:

1. A lawyer to wind things down properly (in most jurisdictions, it must be an attorney)
2. Funding to cover residual overhead and to compensate the person doing the work

This is why, if you own a firm, I *highly* recommend you do the following (and if I could make it mandatory, I would):

- Identify your backup attorney
- Have an open conversation with your backup attorney about your plan
- Get the right agreements and documentation in place
- Secure key person life insurance and a business overhead policy to fund the wind down if needed

This doesn't take long to do. But the peace of mind it brings is worth everything. You'll rest easier knowing that if the worst happens, your clients, your staff, and your family won't be left scrambling. It's one of the most important professional responsibilities you have. And one of the easiest to put off.

So take the time. Put the plan in place. You'll be glad you did. If you're careful and close up responsibly, you can move on to the next phase of your life with confidence.

For me, that phase of life will mean getting back to music—as a performer, but also as a concert promoter. Whether that's organizing private events, festivals, or something entirely new. Sounds crazy, I know, but I want to return to that world that once brought me so much joy.

But I always keep that dream in the back of my mind. When the time comes to close the legal chapter of my life, that's where I'm headed. And maybe that's a reminder for you too.

Think back. What used to light you up? What parts of yourself have been buried under years of work, responsibility, or practicality? Is there a version of that dream you can still pursue? If you plan intentionally and stay connected (or reconnect) to something meaningful beyond your career, that next chapter can be just as fulfilling—maybe even more so.

CONCLUSION

I graduated from college in March 1999. I had gone to an engineering school, and my degree didn't require any foreign language study. Around that time, a friend of mine—also graduating—suggested we travel to Costa Rica after graduation to learn Spanish. It sounded like a great idea, so we made plans to leave in late May.

Then my friend called to let me know he couldn't go. He was scheduled to report to Navy flight school the following January to train as a jet pilot, but the navy moved up his start date to June, and he had to back out of our trip. I told him I was going anyway.

And I did. I went to Costa Rica alone. I enrolled in a language immersion program, lived with a local family, and spent my time traveling and meeting people from all over the world. I barely knew any Spanish when I arrived—just a few phrases I had picked up in the weeks before—but I figured it out as I went.

That experience was a defining moment for me. Going to a foreign country alone, not knowing the language and having to navigate everything on my own, pushed me to grow in ways I hadn't expected. It was one of the most rewarding times of my life, but it was also incredibly challenging, and I never did master Spanish. I learned enough to get around, but I didn't spend enough time in Costa Rica to be fully proficient.

The ins and outs of law firms, though? I have spent enough time on that, so I am fully proficient and really understand the law firm space, although I am still learning new things every day. One advantage I have—indeed, one of my unique selling propositions—is that I have seen so many scenarios that I can bring that breadth of knowledge to every new client engagement. Other lawyers are limited by their own experience or by the experience of those they have consulted (assuming they asked the right questions at all).

Even so, you might think it would be better to figure out the law firm space on your own, and you're not alone. I have noticed that, when it comes to hiring a law firm lawyer, lawyers often fall into distinct camps. Some believe they will never need to hire anyone (*I can figure it out on my own*, they think), some believe they should hire an expert, and some are undecided.

If you think you can do it on your own, I have a message for you. You know you're smart—you're a lawyer. You could figure it out. You could spend lots of time and sort of get to the answer. But because this isn't your main area, you may miss some things. You may get 80 or 90 percent there, but you still may not get all the way there. And you will have spent all that time figuring it out—time that you could be using earning money in your firm.

As a visitor in the "country" of law firm law, do you have that kind of time to spend? Most lawyers don't. And will you get as proficient as someone who has lived in a country for decades? Also probably not.

Some lawyers realize this. They recognize the value of hiring an expert to handle their law firm legal matters. They don't hesitate—they ask. And then there's that large group in the middle that is on the fence about whether they need representation.

Whatever camp you fall into, I encourage you to contact me. I can offer not only a personal perspective but the collective insight gained from watching many people try many approaches and from helping them avoid—or recover from—their mistakes. This is my day-to-day just like your practice area is yours. I can answer your questions, suggest solutions for problems you didn't know about, and help you run your law firm like a well-oiled machine.

My point is, I moved to this "country" long ago. I speak the language like a native. Let me show you around. You can find Jonathan at www.lawfirmgc.com or on LinkedIn.

BIBLIOGRAPHY

Buckner, Susan, and Melissa Bender. "Lawyer Complaints" FindLaw. 2023. https://www.findlaw.com/hirealawyer/ choosing-the-right-lawyer/lawyer-complaints.html.

Ernst & Young. "Are You Giving M&A Integration Costs the Attention They Deserve?" Accessed June 19, 2025. https://www.ey.com/content/dam/ey-unified-site/ey-com/en-cn/insights/strategy-transactions/documents/ ey-integration-costs-mergers-and-acquisitions.pdf.

Greiner, Lori. *Invent It, Sell It, Bank It!: Make Your Million-Dollar Idea into a Reality*. New York: Ballantine Books, 2014.

Henson, Priscilla. "Addiction & Substance Abuse in Lawyers: Statistics to Know," American Addiction Centers. Updated January 28, 2025. https:// americanaddictioncenters.org/workforce-addiction/ white-collar/lawyers.

Karlinsky, Neal, and Jordan Stead. "How a Door Became a Desk, and a Symbol of Amazon." About Amazon, January 17, 2018. https://www.aboutamazon.com/news/workplace/how-a-door-became-a-desk-and-a-symbol-of-amazon.

Moore, Philip J., Nancy E. Adler, and Patricia A. Robertson. "Medical Malpractice: The Effect of Doctor-Patient Relations on Medical Patient Perceptions and Malpractice Intentions." *Western Journal of Medicine* 173, no. 4 (October 2000): 244–50. https://www.ncbi.nlm.nih.gov/pmc/articles/PMC1071103/.

North Carolina State Bar. "2020 Formal Ethics Opinion 1: Responding to Negative Online Reviews." Adopted July 16, 2021. Accessed June 18, 2025. https://www.ncbar.gov/for-lawyers/ethics/adopted-opinions/2020-formal-ethics-opinion-1/.

Rumsfeld, Donald. Interview by Deputy Inspector General for Investigations. Department of Defense. Office of Inspector General. U.S. Department of Defense. April 1, 2005. https://media.defense.gov/2006/Jun/30/2001774458/-1/-1/1/r_FOIA-Release-Rumsfeld-Transcript.pdf.

Rushing, Don G., and Andrew B. Serwin. "Pathways to Wellness in the Practice of Law." *The Bencher*—March/April 2020. American Inns of Court. Accessed June 18, 2025. https://home.innsofcourt.org/AIC/AIC_For_Members/AIC_Bencher/AIC_Bencher_Recent_Articles/2020_MarApr_Rushing-Serwin.aspx.

ABOUT THE AUTHOR

Jonathan Hawkins is a business lawyer for lawyers. As the founder of Law Firm GC, he helps attorneys and law firms navigate the legal challenges of running a practice. He also hosts the *Founding Partner Podcast*, where he interviews law firm founders and shares the lessons they've learned along the way.

Over the years, Jonathan has worked with firms of all sizes. From solo practitioners to organizations with more than two hundred attorneys, from start-ups to those generating nine-figure revenues, he's done it all. His clients span nearly every practice area—personal injury, family law, immigration, criminal defense, insurance, corporate, real estate, employment, estate planning, and even highly specialized niches.

A third-generation Georgia Tech engineer and second-generation lawyer, Jonathan has been recognized as a Top

100 Lawyer in Georgia by Super Lawyers and holds an AV Preeminent Peer Review Rating from Martindale-Hubbell. He lives in Atlanta with his wife and twin teenagers. When he's not working on his business or hanging out with his family, Jonathan spends his time watching college football and going to reggae concerts.